**22 famous
painters
and
illustrators
tell how
they work**

22 famous

painters

and

illustrators

**Invaluable advice
from the
Guiding Faculty of the
Famous Artists Schools,
Westport, Connecticut**

tell how

they work

**David McKay
Company, Inc.
New York**

BY MARY ANNE GUITAR

22 famous
painters
and
illustrators
tell how
they work

Library of Congress Catalog Card Number: 63-19334
Manufactured in the United States of America

Contents

Introduction

By Albert Dorne

The distinguished American painters and illustrators represented in this book share one thing in common. They are all professionals, in the purest meaning of the word. They have all tasted the sweet fruits of success as artists—public recognition, the high regard of their profession and economic security in their work.

In the case of the illustrators, each has been an innovator, creating his own "school" of illustration for others to follow. The painters, too, have been originators of styles and points of view as artists. All have been part of the mainstream of American Art. What they have to say is important not only in the field of Art but also in the culture of our times.

With an average of more than thirty years experience—as professional artists and as teachers of art—they have much to convey to the young painter or illustrator who would develop his knowledge and skill of the craft of drawing and painting into a significant and personal art. They all express with simple candor their opinions on the esthetics and the practical aspects of their art—on their subjective creative needs and their objective purpose as artists.

You won't find agreement on every point among these artists. They have strong personal convictions and their own individual ways of working. It is important for the student of art, however, to be exposed to such diversity of opinion.

In its highest sense, professionalism is a constantly felt dedication to the best—a state of mind which raises the professional far above the mere status of mercenary. Every artist in this book is the true "pro"— a man of conviction and self-imposed goals of high order, a man living out his career with a carefully nurtured vision of perfect performance.

The spectator and non-artist will find in this volume many answers to Art and its meanings, told in the simple language of the practical professional, without the confusing literary obscurities and double-talk that unfortunately constitute so large a part of today's art criticism and opinion.

The serious student whose aspirations are professional (whether in painting or illustration) and the dedicated amateur searching for direction would also do well to read this book thoughtfully.

I'm sure it offers a new dimension for understanding the work and the philosophy of these distinguished painters and illustrators. And even more important, I believe it will affect your own attitude as an artist, no matter what your ultimate goal.

**22 famous
painters
and
illustrators
tell how
they work**

1

WILL BARNET

**22 famous
painters
and
illustrators
tell how
they work**

Photograph of the artist

Will Barnet has made a significant contribution to American art for more than twenty-five years. His disciplined use of form and his use of brilliant colors have won him countless art prizes. Barnet's paintings hang in the Museum of Modern Art, the Corcoran Gallery, the Whitney Museum, the Guggenheim Museum, and many others here and abroad. While restlessly experimenting with abstract painting, Barnet has never abandoned the figure. He likens himself to Dutch painters who sought their subject matter close at hand. Barnet, too, paints mothers and children and the intimate details of domesticity. Writer James Farrell says of his pictures, "These have been painted with a love which almost approaches the possessive . . . In Will Barnet's eyes the commonplace is seen freshly, and with deep affection and sympathy. Through the skill of this devoted artist, the ordinary becomes a new visual world." Born in Beverly, Massachusetts, Barnet studied at the Boston Museum of Fine Arts and later at the Art Students League of New York. He lives in New York City where he teaches at Cooper Union and the Art Students League.

Form and Figure

I have always been interested in the human figure. I painted my parents and family when I was young, and then, when I married, my wife and children became my subjects. My hero was Vermeer who could make a domestic scene represent the entire world. My early and middle work was very much involved with family life and the home. I am basically interested in the human being, and this is what I like to paint.

My abstract period at its best was, I hope, a real statement of feeling for the universe. It reflected my growing concern with the world. I was breaking out of the home into the larger world of man and nature. It was a larger, vaster, more transcendental world. Also, for the first time, strong landscapes entered my work.

The development of an artist is organic. The abstract work was related to the earlier period and, of course, to my current work. My work has always been figurative except during one period when I had taken the figure and integrated parts of it in an abstract way. So I never really left the figure. It simply transformed itself. When I felt the challenge of going back to figurative work, I could do so using all the new concepts I had developed in my abstract work. My painting today reflects the interest of my earlier

3

Creation. Oil. Schaefer Gallery

period in the human character. But a new spirit has
entered my present work. I am now interested in
richly formed monumental movements.

? *Are you conscious of trying to say something original?*

a If you are original, you don't think about originality.
If you feel something intensely, and you say it with
enough energy, it becomes original. It belongs to you,
and it is you.

? *The people in your paintings today are recognizable
human beings, and yet they seem symbolic, rather than
realistic. Do they represent certain ideas you have of
the world?*

4

**Will
Barnet**

a I like to call what I am doing today "abstract reality."
My people are identifiable. They are real people, and
I work from live models. But I try to go beyond the
temporary associations we have with human beings so
that people of all ages and periods will enjoy them.
There is concern for the personality of the person I am
painting, but the proportions are transformed, the
sizes are reframed. They are meant to represent a
larger feeling because my work is not just intimate
portraiture. Some people think of my portraits as
having an Oriental quality but this is due to the fact
that most Occidental portraiture has no abstract
element.

I don't believe that anything is really abstract in
the sense that it has no connection with reality.
I believe the word is put to better use if you think of
abstraction as a way of transforming forms in painting
so that they become abstract. The abstract quality
comes out in the way the forms are cultivated and
directed. No matter what kind of painting you do
today you deal with reality. The way you handle that
reality makes it more abstract or less abstract.

Realistic art can be abstract. The art of a man like
Ingres has a certain feeling for physical reality, but
at the same time, the transformation of the shapes and
forms is an abstraction.

? *Your paintings have a formality, an intellectual
quality about them. Is this a calculated effect?*

a I tend to have mixed feelings about a subject, part
emotional and part analytical. It's the complexity
that fascinates me. When I get into the subject, I try
to find out what makes it work. I try to find the
essential quality of it, the basic quality. It is a
long, drawn-out process where the thing goes through
many stages. The last stage is the most inspiring of
all—the final revelation of the idea. A good deal
of feeling goes into the work. I don't lose my
inspiration. My inspiration becomes greater as I paint.
I begin slowly. I think painting has to ripen. I'm not
very interested in immediacy. I often work for months
on a picture and put it away after a while if I don't
resolve it. Every painting I do requires at least several
months of work. Of course, I can be planning another
painting during that time, or thinking about it.

I work from a preliminary sketch, or many
preliminary sketches, which is very important.
I couldn't work from one that didn't show real promise.
The sketch is what I call the "action step." But as the

Singular Image. Oil. Schaefer Gallery

work progresses it must be continually reconsidered in terms of the form. The original idea is kept even though the form may be changed a great deal. I would say that my original idea is crystallized in a more binding form rather than changed. I transform the original idea, but the germ remains and I make the most of it.

I think you should paint any subject that interests you. People who love to paint flowers should paint flowers as much as théy like. Those who like to paint people should paint people. Those who like landscapes should paint them. The subject is important up to a point, but beyond that is the way you interpret it aesthetically. It isn't the subject that makes the picture important, but the way the subject is painted.

How you handle form and color adds, of course, to the interest of the subject.

You have to understand the visual elements of painting. To me, such concepts as form and color have very specific identifications. Form, for example, to me means a plane that begins to describe the position of an object. The first thing I touch with my brush or pencil is a plane, specifically the tightly stretched canvas. That's a plane to me. All my thoughts are centered on how to work with this plane. It has a beginning and an end, and I have to work within its limitations.

**? ** *Form, to you then, is the basic visual element?*

a Color is very important, too—but I still think that form is the very essence of painting and color the final binder. Many of the art historians write about Cézanne and how he got his form through color. Why, then, is he so good in black and white? The color is beautifully integrated with the form, but you wouldn't find his work so impressive if the form weren't right. Form to me is character. I don't like an anonymous kind of drawing. Good work should give the feeling that you live in the world, that you have had contact with reality. Form does that.

The artist should appreciate the complexities of line and drawing. If a man is serious, he tries to find out the essence, the basic character of an object. He tries to work with this and not get immediately involved with details. In other words, he tries to get a clear idea of how the basic forms work. Each picture is a search. It's like starting all over again. It has a freshness. Beauty for me has a certain final association of things working together. It is the highest form of art— this search for relationships—and it is the thing that drives me on.

I think drawing is major. Of course, the attitude about drawing has changed since I was a student. Even in those days, however, drawing was not just literal copying. Each artist when he made a drawing interpreted it from a certain point of view. Today, artists interpret from another point of view. Good drawing today demands a great facility for the kind of observation that incorporates the whole world, not just descriptive skill but a certain ability to put objects in relation to one another. What I felt as a student was a lack of interrelatedness. We didn't learn how to put things together. One of the errors of that period was that we learned to draw one thing at a time and

**Will
Barnet**

Sleeping Child. Oil. Collection of the artist

weren't taught what each thing meant in relation to something else. Drawing today has a much wider meaning—the ability to give things a relatedness.

? *Your early training at the Boston Museum was in the tradition of the French Academy with its emphasis on discipline, wasn't it?*

a Oh yes. I took the museum's four-year course, and I worked all the time. In those days, you had to have a year of cast drawing and that meant sitting there all morning and studying the casts of great classical heads.

I loved the grand statuary. Our teachers were absolute perfectionists, and we had to copy those statues down to the last curl. I remember having my first disagreement with one of the instructors when I had done a head with only twenty-six curls, and he counted twenty-seven on the cast!

I would do it all over again but with certain modifications. When I look back, I think it was a marvelous experience. I would include some of the stiff courses they had. We weren't allowed to paint until the fourth year. I would change this and introduce it early in the program.

I came in at the end of an era. I was taught by the last generation that truly belonged to the French Academy. But during the formative years when I was going to school, the art of the great French Impressionist period was flowing into this country. And this made me aware of another school of art.

? *What personal qualities are important to the painter?*

a In order to be a painter, you need more than talent. This is not an original statement, but it is true. You must put in 97 per cent sweat and 3 per cent talent to produce a success. A man like Rubens, however, had great talent. In his case, it was probably 50 per cent inspiration and 50 per cent perspiration.

The artist must have the ability to bring a visual perception into focus. He has to be able to think in visual terms.

? *Can this be taught?*

a I think it can be cultivated. That is why I teach. I really believe that some people have a greater capacity to perceive than others. But you can learn to see. You need a certain sympathy for art and a respect for visual images. This aids learning. You can benefit by the experiences of the past, and this is why study is so important. I don't believe nature changes. It has its laws, and you have to respect them. By learning to live with them, you can be creative. You have to be able to think of life as being a continuous process. This is part of what you should feel if you want to be a creative person. You have to be taught to see the world. Maybe we are able to see it right when we're young, but this perception must be cultivated when we grow older.

Father and Son. Oil. Collection of Mr. and Mrs. M. L. Mattlin

? *All of your life has been spent with art, studying it, teaching it, and creating it. Did you plan to become this involved, or did you accidentally stumble into the world of art?*

a I never wanted to be anything but an artist. I was determined to be an artist, and I was old enough at five to speak up for my rights. Everybody just had to accept my choice. As a matter of fact, no one in my family painted or talked about pictures. But I had a sympathetic mother who encouraged me. Art always attracted me. It was in my nature to enjoy certain

visual things. You might say I was born an artist in
that sense. But, of course, I've had to struggle to
fulfill my ambitions and become a painter.

I was brought up in a rural New England
environment. The library was the only source of
culture, but, fortunately for me, it contained a large
number of art books. I used to take out books of
Watteau's paintings when I was eight or nine years old
and copy his work. Rembrandt's drawings also made
a great impression on me.

Today, Modigliani, Léger, Juan Gris would be
among the first I would choose if I could afford to
collect them. Or, I would like to have a good painting
by Picasso—but it would have to be something he did
at least twenty years ago. I like Stuart Davis very
much, and certain other contemporaries of mine.

? *Could you analyze what made you want to paint?*

a One of the things that made me become a painter was
the need to give a certain permanence to living. I felt
life was very fragile. There are certain moments in
life you want to hang on to, and by painting them,
you can give these moments a kind of immortality.
There is no guarantee that what you do will survive,
but at least you are fulfilling what I believe is the
artist's responsibility to define, select, and emphasize
experiences that the ordinary man might pass by or
accept too easily. Each generation of artists finds
fresh things in nature, things nobody has found
before. The artist has a special role in society. He is
saying, in a sense, "Maybe we're walking too fast. I'm
stopping for a moment to examine this experience."
It is up to him to reveal things that other people
might miss.

I think art's great contribution is the ennobling of
man. Great art lifts you up. Throughout the ages, man
has conquered tragedy with his ability to create a work
of art.

? *Could you give us an example of what you mean by a
lasting value, one that has its roots in the past but
that is still significant today?*

a I would say that a respect for living things is all
important today and has been important to the great
artists of the past. This is what I would like to
illuminate in my own work, and when I succeed in
doing so, I feel very happy. This is what makes
painting so immensely rewarding and exciting.

2

ARNOLD BLANCH

**22 famous
painters
and
illustrators
tell how
they work**

Photograph of the artist

Arnold Blanch is one of the best known painters in America. His book illustrations, paintings, designs, and ceramics are the fruit of forty years' work. These achievements have brought him innumerable prizes and awards from art critics. His paintings hang in seventeen public collections, including the Metropolitan Museum, the Whitney Museum, the Carnegie Institute and the Library of Congress. Blanch was born in Mantorville, Minnesota. A disinterested student, he quit school at the age of fourteen and enrolled in the Minneapolis School of Art. Later, he attended the Art Students League in New York City on a scholarship. There he studied under John Sloan and Robert Henri. In 1933, Blanch won a Guggenheim Fellowship and this enabled him to travel in Europe and paint full time. He has never stopped painting, or traveling about the world. When he is not in residence at Woodstock, New York, where he shares a studio-home with his wife, artist Doris Lee, he can be found in Europe or Florida.

A devoted teacher, Blanch has influenced students at the University of Minnesota, Ohio State, the University of Hawaii, the Art Students League, and other institutions.

Joy of Painting

I think my greatest satisfaction as a person as well as an artist is to be able to get up in the morning and say to myself I have nothing to do today but work. In other occupations, most people think of work simply as something to do until they have accumulated enough money to retire. The artist works to be able to keep on working at what he loves best.

? *You came from a family of practicing artists so I suppose you discovered this love of painting at an early age. Is this why you became an artist?*

a I think I became an artist because during the early part of my life, I discovered that ordinary language was insufficient for the images I wished to communicate. I entered the profession as a sort of romantic child, but I soon found that it is a very difficult profession if you want to earn a living and satisfy yourself with your paintings. It's hard work, but I think you've got to like hard work to become a painter. I've had a very rich life. I have traveled to all parts of the world and met many wonderful people. The fun of it has been

Birds. Casein. Collection of Emily Wellson

tremendous. I don't think I'd ever trade it for any other life.

? *Do you have a philosophy as an artist, one that has perhaps evolved during the many years you have been painting and teaching art?*

a I don't know that you can call it a philosophy, but I have a very strong feeling about art. When I visit a certain chapel abroad, one that has marvelous paintings on its walls, I experience a sort of elation and pride in being an artist, in belonging to a profession that could produce art like this. It touches me very deeply. No doubt the painter's subject was more important. The style is there, but the many people who come from all over the world to look at these paintings are getting some quality, some feeling from the picture. The artist has done this wonderful thing for them.

? *Are you trying to communicate through your paintings the joy you find in art?*

a I think first one communicates with himself. You have something. You don't know what it is, but you want to see what it is. If you like it, you want to share it with others. I know at this stage of my life, now that I've had a lot of experience, the first thing I ask myself when I begin a picture is, who will I share this with? Who will enjoy it? I feel that artists do want to communicate with others, but I don't think this is the fundamental reason why we paint.

Arnold Blanch

? *What is your own primary reason for painting, then?*

a To bring forth. I don't know what I'm going to bring forth until it's been visualized, but it's there and I want to give it life. Through the act of painting, we can add new dimension to our everyday life and make visible our love for the world around us. You just can't set out to make a good work of art. You set out to make something and enjoy making it. Art is an experiment, and some of these experiments will turn out to be unusual paintings. I think it's a good thing that we have so many artists working today. Out of this large group, some will become good artists. In much the same way, some of the many boys who play baseball will become good ballplayers. Now there are those who say that the general standard of art will be lowered because so many are now practicing artists. I say there will be greater heights reached because more are reaching for the heights.

? *Why do you draw and paint as you do? Your paintings of the thirties have a look far different from the work you are doing today, or did ten years ago.*

a I have been painting for forty years, and the years have passed all too quickly. During this time, the face of my painting has often changed. The influences that contributed to the changes were both historical and current. I like to believe that under the surface of time and change there have been dominant values established. For these values, I owe great thanks to Emerson, Melville, Thoreau, Freud, the Old and New Testaments, and all the music and poetry ever written. The fact that I live in the country and love the country has to do with them. Even my relationship with people has to do with them. My students have perhaps influenced me more than I've influenced them.

? *Can you explain why?*

a Artists tend to become overinvolved in the good things of life after they become successful. Such things as domesticity and suburban living. My association with

Red Landscape. Casein and oil. Collection of Eleanor Lowenthal

students has perhaps made me believe that these things are not important and that dedication is important. A student doesn't usually have these material things so he is able to give his whole life to his work.

? *What experiences, training, emotional impulses impel you to choose the subjects you are fond of painting?*

a It has to do with my feeling for the sky and growing things and people and the sea and changing seasons. These are the things I really believe in. This is my religious belief. The process of life is much more mysterious and awe-inspiring than anything man has created. The process of life and death is such a terrific thing. One of the things I like about bread is that it is alive. Now, I don't think I try to communicate my feeling about these things by saying the earth is warm in summer and cold in winter. But because I love these things, I try to glorify them in my painting. Sometimes, of course, an artist may hate things and be bitter, and that's justifiable, too. I feel very bitter about war, and I think if I were younger I'd be more bitter.

? *How deliberately do you plan a picture, and how deliberate are you in actually making one?*

a I makes lots of drawings from the objects around me, from flowers and trees, the sea and the mountains.

Arnold Blanch

Often I follow the drawings when I start to paint, but sometimes I don't. When you make a note on paper or in your mind, you don't necessarily have to refer to it again because its essence runs in your memory. I tend to work in a series of pictures. I get involved with some sort of an image, let us say. I'm not satisfied with one painting of it, and so I do several—the first being the source of the second and the second, the source of the third. While I'm drawing, I'm never critical. I'm critical afterward. If I'm critical while I'm working, it will show. You draw to the best of your ability. It must have a security about it, an authority, an authenticity.

? *Do you experiment while you are working, or do you see the end result of a painting before you start on it?*

a I don't have a visual image of the result I want to achieve, but I do have a sort of feeling. I might say that one day I feel like a cool painting, using cool colors. The next day the feeling changes, and I have a strong desire to make a warm painting with warm colors. Usually I start a painting in either a high key or a low key. This feeling of mine usually precedes the painting, but I may change feelings in the middle of the picture. A painter is an inventive person. Through experimentation, he finds ways of doing things. In some cases, these are shortcuts: at other times, they are the opposite of shortcuts. Each painter must find ways of achieving his own ends rather than accepting the traditional means of doing things.

? *Then your first response to a subject is more emotional than intellectual or analytical?*

a I think we all see in a rather arbitrary way, depending upon our individual feelings. For example, I am doing a lot of red pictures of the ocean now. The ocean is never red, but I like the idea of a red ocean. My pictures are not intended to be exact, documentary reproductions of the ocean as it really looks. But I am making the ocean red because I like the idea. It's purely subjective on my part. Also, after looking at so many paintings over the years, I have discovered that one gets a little bored with the conventional reproductions of nature—the blue sky and green tree sort of thing. When the artist adds his nature to the nature outside himself, there is a greater accumulation of feeling in the picture. The nature of painting itself also comes into it. What is contemporary and current. This also influences the painter.

Circus Girl. Oil. Art Students League of New York

? *Do you mean that the painter must constantly strive to keep up with the times and be original?*

a If a person is an original person, this will come out. And, of course, most painters who have had any achievements are creative and original. But when originality is consciously sought, even if it is achieved, it dies very quickly. There is a lot of painting today where uniqueness has been strived for. It becomes old very quickly.

? Do you ever have trouble deciding what to paint?

a The problem of deciding what to paint is a continuous
and perennial one. Corot said, "When I sit before
that white canvas, I feel that I've never painted before."
I don't think you can worry about what is an interesting
subject to paint. You have to find it for yourself. You
might go out tomorrow and see a terrific subject in
the branch of a tree. Perhaps you hadn't noticed it
before. You can't force this kind of thing, but it
will come if you work all the time at your painting.
Young painters have said to me from time to time,
"I think if I could work more steadily my painting
would be better. There is always something that gets
in the way." All of us have had this problem. The light
is bad. The canvas needs stretching. The brushes
aren't clean. These small discouragements can be
avoided if you have a private place (not necessarily a
large one) to store your tools and materials and keep
them in condition. The important thing is always to
paint and avoid postponement; therefore, your
equipment should always be in order. However,
I believe the greatest inhibitor is the fear that you
aren't going to be able to paint something great. All
too often the student is too anxious to produce a
work of art. A work of art is the by-product of the love
of painting.

**? Well, suppose the student finds a subject that attracts
him. How does he decide it is one worth painting?**

a The inexperienced painter will often prevent himself
from working by pursuing a futile search for the
perfect subject. Anything that interests a painter is
worthwhile. Look at Van Gogh. He painted shoes.
Rembrandt painted a side of beef. The subject matter
doesn't make a picture, it's artistry that counts.

**? How should he approach his subject once he has been
attracted to it and has decided to make a painting?**

a Certainly he should not merely copy the subject.
Sometimes students will look at a model and trace it.
A Rembrandt would look at a model and produce
something that had a life of its own. He would not
think of copying it but would instead give it a new
life. The model had given him something. This had
gone through him, so to speak, and now he wants to
give it back. I think of a painting as something that

Arnold
Blanch

19

Unicef Card. Casein

has to live, in the same way a person has to live. Of course, each person will approach a painting in a different way. One may know exactly what he wants from the start. Another may not. For myself, I establish what it is possible to do. Delacroix once said, "You start a painting with a broom and finish with a needle." This precisely describes my method.

? *What should the student artist know and learn about making pictures?*

a He should know everything possible about art. The greater his studiousness, the greater the chance of developing his potential as an artist, if there is talent. He should also know his subject. He learns about it best by painting it many times, adjusting it in many ways. It isn't only a matter of knowing the subject, however. He must make it part of the space he's working with. A canvas is often thought of as something you paint on instead of a dynamic thing in itself. You can't add to it or destroy it, but you can glorify it. All too often students will buy a canvas, say a square canvas, and paint an oblong picture. The picture must look as if it belongs on nothing but a

square. Of course, it can be done by painting it over
and over again. I make maybe five or ten paintings of
a subject before I arrive at something that pleases me
to any degree.

**Arnold
Blanch**

? *Often the painter has learned his craft and feels secure
in it. What is most important as an element in making
pictures—emotion, intellect, or skill?*

a I don't really know how to separate emotion and
intellect. They are all mixed up in me. Certainly
skill is important, but it becomes second nature after
you have been painting for a long time. What the artist
probably feels for his painting is empathy. He gets so
involved in the picture. There is a peculiar state of
mind that exists in painting. You paint for an hour or
so, and you're suddenly drained of energy. You feel as
though you've gone through some emotional upheaval.
It is total involvement. Sometimes there is a certain
amount of anger generated by the involvement. This
may be essential because it indicates that a great
creative effort has been made. Often the paintings of a
facile artist will lack visual excitement because he hasn't
fought his way through to a personal resolution.

? *How important is drawing to the total result of the
picture?*

a Painting is only an extension of drawing. Drawing is
the means by which the painter rehearses. He trains his
eye, hand, and nervous system. This is the instrument
by which we become skillful, and it is the area in
which we can experiment. One way to be sure you have
a continuous supply of subjects that can be developed
into paintings is to keep a sketchbook filled with
drawings, drawings of almost anything.

? *You had a rather formal art training—at the
Minneapolis School of Art and one term at the Art
Students League where you studied under John Sloan
and Robert Henri. Would you choose a different kind
if you were starting over again?*

a No. But then I have never really stopped studying.
I am happy when I am learning, and there is always
something to learn. I have a book of sketches by
Picasso. You leaf through it and find sketch after
sketch brilliantly conceived by Picasso. Then, suddenly
he stops and copies a Rembrandt. This is the secret of
this man's tremendous gifts. He never thought he was

through learning. He could still get something from Rembrandt. I've been teaching for thirty years, and I'm still amazed at what can be learned. The process of learning never stops, and we learn so much by experience.

? *What do you look for in a picture?*

**Arnold
Blanch**

a In looking at a picture, I very seldom look at it in terms of learning how it was done. If it attracts me, it rises above the means by which it was done, even though I might later become a teacher or student and study it from the point of view of its structure.

? *How do you feel about abstract art?*

a Often the abstract painters are trying to find something that is not hackneyed, trying to find a new subject, maybe a new form, but certainly not something you can always put into words. I think the content of a painting is very important although I don't always know how to pin it down to words. I lecture a lot and sometimes find it very difficult to explain the content of a picture to people who have not seen much abstract art. Recently, I was talking to a group of older people, and we were discussing a painting that was abstract. They asked me if it was supposed to be a town. I said, no, it is not supposed to be a town. A painting is like a seed. It grows into something else, a plant, a flower, depending upon you. They asked me why I couldn't explain what I liked about the painting. I answered that there are a lot of things that are nonverbal. For example, most people have eaten an egg. Can they tell me what an egg tastes like? It is very hard to say what the content of a picture is, even though the subject matter is obvious. Here is a picture of Doris Lee, my wife, by Milton Avery. But it's not of her, really. It's some kind of visual experience we can all enjoy without necessarily understanding it.

? *What kind of enjoyment do you expect to get out of a picture?*

a When I go to the Metropolitan Museum, I walk through the halls and sometimes I stop in front of a picture and sometimes I pass it by. I go through with an open mind, not hunting for anything in particular. I think a painting has to like you if you like the painting. There has to be some kind of mutual exchange. A painting that stops you, calls attention to itself, has qualities that sort of seek you out. The same thing happens with people.

? *What principal advice would you give to a student?*

a I would tell him that he has to learn to be very tough. The creative person is sensitive, very sensitive to destructive things so he has to be able to survive not only the acclaim of an audience but also survive their ignoring him. If you can survive both things, you have proven yourself. Some can survive the neglect but not the acclaim. The life of a painter moves in periods. At first, when you get involved in the work, you feel depressed because you have to deprive yourself. You feel isolated from society. You are creating a language not many people understand. Your parents look at your work oddly. Some people can't live through this. Then, a little later on, there is the battle against the social form of success. The creative person needs isolation and this isolation can be disturbing. Then you realize that through this thing you are working on, you are deepening yourself. Some part of the world comes to you. At times God is very good to those who are talented, and people do things for those who are gifted. Talent opens many doors. There is respect for it. So you don't feel depressed any more. You willingly sacrifice the worldly pleasure and enjoy the pleasure you get out of working.

? *What factors besides talent are important to an artist?*

a I was one of those talented students who always got scholarships. But you can't lean on your talent. You can't use it as a crutch. Some students lean on it too heavily. The talented student knows he can do something people will "oh" and "ah" at, so he's easily satisfied. He doesn't struggle with it. I wish I could help every student realize that he must possess more than talent if he wants to be a good painter. It takes great skill and experience to be free, spontaneous, all those things a painter would like to be. We would all like to have a piece of art happen as spontaneously as a bird flying. A painting may seem to have been created with much freedom, but the freedom has only been accomplished through the discipline of experience. You must exact from yourself great energy, sensitivity, and ability. The will and incentive to reach out to further insight and growth is most rare, yet it is this quality that is the most rewarding.

3

AUSTIN BRIGGS

**22 famous
painters
and
illustrators
tell how
they work**

Photograph of the artist

Austin Briggs is fond of quoting Henry James's advice to writers—"Try to be one of the people on whom nothing is lost." Briggs himself has followed this advice throughout his career as an illustrator; he is an acute and sensitive observer of the contemporary scene. In addition to countless advertising and magazine illustrations, Briggs has done television work, posters, billboards, and book illustrations; he has designed a stock certificate, a record album, and even a match cover. He paints in virtually every medium. Born in Humboldt, Minnesota, Briggs started on his art career at an early age. When he was sixteen his pictures were appearing in Detroit newspaper advertisements. In 1927 he began doing illustrations for the Dearborn *Independent,* and a year later *Collier's* published his work. Briggs and his wife Ellen moved to New York on the strength of the *Collier's* sale. For three years Briggs sold to the leading magazines of the day and then, abruptly, the sale stopped. He was twenty-three at the time and the country was in the depths of the depression. Characteristically, however, Briggs blames his decline on himself and not hard times. "I realized I just wasn't doing acceptable work," he says about this period. He began a Spartan-like retraining period in which he developed the strength and style which has put him at the top of his profession. His honesty about himself and his craft has made him one of the country's most respected illustrators.

The Contemporary Look

I'm interested in being as truthful as I can be in showing aspects of our culture. What I am interested in doing most of all is expressing the instantaneous look of the people in our time who are the busiest at whatever they are doing. The greatest compliment on my work was paid me by John Updike, the writer, who told me I was able to express accurately the feel and look of people of today.

The people in the advertising series I did for *TV Guide* are the successes, the powerful people, but I am attempting to be very truthful about them. I have not idealized them in any way. For example, there's a certain reverse snobbery in their Ivy League look. John Updike recognized what I was trying to do when he said that in my drawings "Madison Avenue personnel were captured in all their dapper fatigue." Interestingly enough, the more I emphasized these qualities, the more the subjects liked the drawings. I think the artist must be of the people but standing a

With his eerie smile, Ronald Marrone stood apart from the lively teen-age world. And Starr Zeitler possessed everything he lacked—good looks, vivacity, popularity.

The Strange Boy. Brush and ink. *Look,* August 5, 1958

little aside. True, I feel a real empathy toward these people, but I am not one of them. I don't view them with any hostility at all. I see them, and myself, too, as being made by our environment to a great extent.

I did not suggest the idea of the *TV Guide* series. An advertising agency in Philadelphia called me up and said they wanted to do three ads showing advertising people in their native habitat. Perhaps they would be in the office of an agency or on the streets of New York, Chicago, or San Francisco, dressed in what seemed to be their "uniform." They were to be engaged in conversation. The target of the ads, of course, was the advertising people who bought space in *TV Guide.* I had never had an assignment that interested me so much, although I have had some fascinating ones.

Some years ago, I was one of a group of artists and idea people who advised a Detroit agency on an automobile account. During a five-year period, I got to know these people so intimately in working situations that I understood them as well as I understand anybody outside of my fellow artists. Fortunately, I have a very good memory for fleeting action. I can, for example, remember some of the things my wife does around the garden and years later put these motions into a picture. So when the *TV Guide* series came up, I was anxious to do it because I knew these people so well.

It is the most successful campaign I have ever had anything to do with. Not long ago, I started working on my fortieth *TV Guide* ad. In the years I have been doing the series, their advertising revenue has gone up every year. A great deal of credit should go to Elmer Pizzi, one of the finest art directors I've ever worked for.

Austin Briggs

If the campaign had been done dishonestly, it would have been just as unsuccessful as all those other campaigns that set out to flatter the advertising industry. I had one ad that showed three people talking in an office. One man was having his shoes shined. He was so engrossed with the problem at hand that he was completely unaware of the shoeshiner at work. Typically, one of the others would probably pay for the service.

? *Do you feel that the demands of the commercial world are restrictive? Are you ever bound to conventional attitudes and ways of presenting an idea?*

a Commercial demands are great. I think the question of how restricted you are depends on each individual assignment. Sometimes one finds an opportunity to speak in a picture very directly because the picture demands it. Other times the picture portrays a view of life at odds with me. Then the picture is usually phony.

I had a lot of trouble once with the picture I did of a small boy leaning over the rail of a ship at sea. The advertising agency thought people would be apprehensive about it and be afraid he would fall overboard. Finally the picture went to the president of the company, and he was convinced that it would do what I wanted the series to do—make people believe it was fun to take this trip.

? *Do you have to have a personal feeling for a commercial assignment before you can approach it with enthusiasm?*

a Of course the feeling for the subject must be there. In magazine illustration, for instance, you have to have empathy for the characters in the story; that is, you have to know how they feel. But the picture changes as I work on it. I was working on an

TV Guide. Carbon stick

illustration for *McCall's* recently. The scene of the
story was a New York City brownstone. I went to New
York and looked at a hodgepodge of buildings, even
though I knew the locale of the story quite well.
I don't think the readers of this kind of fiction are
interested in a literal rendition of a neighborhood.
So I decided to do something quite different. Quite
spontaneously I decided to do my brownstone in
silverpoint. Then I covered it with watercolor.
I achieved a result that was quite appropriate to the
romantic mood of the story. If anybody had asked me
at the beginning if I was going to do it in silverpoint,
I would most certainly have said "no."

   I think empathy is terribly important, the emotional
feel for the subject. You can always master the skills
if you have the desire to do so. If you are hostile to

**Austin
Briggs**

a subject, it doesn't seem to me that you can feel much empathy with it. A picture, in the final analysis, is a synthesis of feeling, intellectual craft, and passion.

Using a camera to save models' fees while you experiment with many different poses is a great convenience. But the camera cannot be used as a substitute for drawing. You cannot draw from a photograph without thought or feeling. There is also a danger in becoming used to one-eyed vision so that you fail to appreciate the value or the experience of seeing with two.

? *You have said that the fundamentals of a good picture are good drawing, good order, good shapes and their arrangement. Is that all?*

a These fundamentals do exist. They are not absolutes. Anyone could make any kind of list of fundamentals. Given enough talent an artist could come along and ignore them all and still do something good. The fundamental I would emphasize is the ability to be able to do what you want to do. If it's a painting you want to make, then you have to know how to paint. If it's a drawing, you must know how to draw. This fundamental is so obvious it is often resisted by students. You can learn any specific craft if you have the desire for it. The desire is the important thing. The important thing is to conceive the picture. It never seemed difficult to me to learn to use a medium if I needed it for a picture.

If I had to start over again, I would choose the most classic and disciplined kind of training possible. I have difficulty with all sorts of things on the craft level that I feel I should not have difficulty with. I make the broad assumption that I can do anything even though very often I can't.

? *What artist most influenced you in your development?*

a I would say Vuillard. He was interested in the setting. And so am I. However, I am much more attracted to sculpture than painting. Calder and Henry Moore are favorites. I have begun in the last few years to buy sculpture I like. My all-time favorite painters are Uccello, Della Francesca, Bonnard, and Vuillard.

? *What factors are important to an illustrator if he is to become a success?*

a Of course you simply have to have talent. You have to be a person, have something to say. The more

Illustration. Tempera. *McCall's*

understanding you have of what we know about life
and the relationships of people to people, the better.

If a student practices over and over doing what he
can do and not what he can't do, he doesn't make
much progress. But if he tries to reach for something
different he will grow as an artist. I never look for
a scene that will be easy (or for that matter,
difficult). I look for something I have a personal
interest in and then try to make it come off.

Experimental art provides the artist with a great
sense of accomplishment. I get part of my satisfaction
in using different mediums. There is far less
difference between fine art and commercial art than
people believe. I'm convinced of this. More and
more, fine artists are painting to order today as did
Michelangelo and Rubens.

? *Conversely, would you say that the commercial artist
has an opportunity today to defy old clichés and
work more freely than in the past?*

a Yes. We are living in a time when mass taste is ready
and asking for change. The American public has been

exposed to more good art, good music, and good reading in recent years than ever before. They're hungry for new aesthetic experiences.

I think the artist is, first of all, an eye. And he must give the public an original and striking and informative message.

Austin Briggs

? *Have you ever had trouble finding a subject to draw or paint?*

a If something interests you, then you should paint it. This is the only thing to consider. I never was any good at all until I realized that the pictures I saw in galleries were done by people who thought it was worth going to all the trouble involved to make a picture out of what they saw. If the painter of flowers in a vase is moved by a subject such as this, it is reason enough for him to paint it. I looked at paintings for years before I realized that they represented a deep interest in the subject on the part of the painter.

? *What attracts you most in a picture?*

a I look for two things—the absolutely familiar and as unique a representation of it as I can find. An umbrella, for example, is just an umbrella. But as Al Parker once said, you get something a little unique if you partially close the umbrella or set it upside down. It gains attention value.

A picture's purpose is to communicate a feeling, a fact, an idea, or a situation that cannot be expressed as well in any other medium.

Truth actually makes a picture, truth and a sense of order. The best picture is the one that suggests, in the final analysis, the greatest order. There are different levels of order just as there is a difference between a simple mind and a complicated mind. If you take a Uccello and cut it up into tiny pieces, you will find order in each square even though they are postage-stamp size.

? *You are called a "hot" artist now. Why do you think your work is in such demand?*

a I think there are three reasons. First, and most importantly, I guess I have been fortunate enough to possess more talent than I thought I had. Second, I have apparently had a continuous development in the quality of my work. When we founded the Famous Artists Schools, I had hardly begun, while the others had found the peak of their form. This makes me look better than I really am because I was farther behind to

31

Elk Hunt. Mixed media. *Sports Illustrated*

begin with. It's like watching a hundred-yard dash in a
track meet. The man who gets a slow start but ends
up with the leaders looks as if he had gone faster than
he has. His performance looks pretty remarkable.
Third, I think I have recognized that aspect of
commercial art I am most interested in and have
found a market for it.

? *You spoke of having more talent than you thought you
possessed. But you have learned how to handle just
about any assignment. What was the most important
period for you in developing your craft?*

**Austin
Briggs**

a The years I spent working for the old *Blue Book* were invaluable to me. I think the stuff I did was awful, but it was different. In those years, I was trying to learn, and the *Blue Book* editor Don Kennicott allowed me to experiment. He respected the potential he saw. He paid me practically nothing, but between the two of us we worked out something good. I could do about any kind of picture for him, and he would accept it. When I finally began getting things in the *Saturday Evening Post,* they asked me for a biographical sketch. I told them Don had influenced me most as an artist. When he read this, he called me up and said, "Well, I finally made the *Saturday Evening Post.*"

? *What excites you most in your working life as an illustrator?*

a The most important thing is that I am communicating. There is something about any artist that makes him want to make a comment on what he sees. My wife is in many ways extraordinarily observant. But she feels no great desire to communicate this to the world. I see something that interests me greatly and want very much to tell other people what I see. It may, as a matter of fact, be an admission that I can't enjoy it all by myself. I try to say to people, "Look at that. Isn't it great? Isn't it fun? Isn't it exciting to look at?"

? *You have achieved a certain reputation and considerable income as an illustrator. Tell me, did you choose this profession because these were the goals you set for yourself?*

a I'm not an illustrator because I hoped to become rich and famous. I have garnered some fame, and I live in a way I never imagined possible. I feel I have some talent, but I take pride in having tried to do as much with it as I could. I don't think my talent is great, but I have used it as well as I can. The good life is a by-product of doing something of high quality that is in demand.

I would like to be, if I could manage it, truly in accord with life. I would like to be a "yea sayer," an approver, enjoying my senses, my mind, my work. One does not have to think of life as perfect to be interested in it, have fun with it, and be excited by it.

4

STUART DAVIS

**22 famous
painters
and
illustrators
tell how
they work**

Photograph of the artist

Someone once commented on a Stuart Davis picture by saying, "You can't miss recognizing a painting by Davis. He is always himself." Davis himself insists, "I paint paintings like mine." Resolutely experimental, Stuart Davis is always a highly recognizable and individual voice. He has never yielded to fads in painting, but has instead pursued his own personal course. He has received countless awards for his work, among them the Guggenheim Fellowship; the Fine Arts Gold Medal of the American Institute of Architects, 1960; election as member of the National Institute of Arts and Letters, 1956; and the Fine Arts Award for Painting, Brandeis University, 1957. His paintings are exhibited in the Museum of Modern Art, the Whitney Museum, the Carnegie Institute, the Art Institute of Chicago, the Metropolitan Museum, and a dozen or more university and college museums.

Born in Philadelphia, Stuart Davis grew up in East Orange, New Jersey. Both his parents were artists and from childhood he associated with their painter friends. When he was sixteen, he abandoned his formal education and began studying with Robert Henri. After serving with Army Intelligence in World War I, Davis sketched and painted while living in Cuba, New Mexico, and Paris. For many years he has lived in New York City, where he appreciates the chance to be near the jazz musicians he counts as his good friends.

Abstract Art

Everybody has originality. It's developed through work. The person has to be himself. The development of self is the achievement of originality. Some people don't seem to want to be themselves.

? *Have you ever wanted to be somebody else?*

a I'm sure I must have, but I forget who. You find out you can't, so you resume being yourself.

? *Would you say that abstract art has a function?*

a Abstract art is so commonplace today and widely accepted that people recognize its excitement. Let me say that the purpose of so-called abstract art is basically the same as all other art and that it always has a subject matter. Mondrian's purpose, for example, is to make a statement of his spiritual experience. Common experience with form, color, and space in

The Terminal. Oil. The Joseph H. Hirshhorn Collection

nature is the subject matter of his art, made explicit in the terms of a logical visual system.

In general, realistic art is art in which the images identify easily with familiar ones.

?   *What do you personally seek in a picture? What excites you?*

a   I look for a complete and balanced subject. By this I mean the picture in its totality, not something outside the picture. The balance means completeness, and completeness means balance. This is the primary consideration. This is not something I look for consciously—it's an automatic response. And since, at one time or another, I've looked at many great pictures of all kinds, I know if the picture is in the tradition of first-class work or not. If it is, it holds your attention. It's a new comment, a new statement in the modern tradition of good art, and you believe it. That's all I respond to. Certainly not to subject matter or the medium or size.

Except that it's impossible to state these things categorically, I would say balance and completeness make a picture. This can happen in a hundred thousand different ways. You can put a line down the middle of a page and you are making a picture, but

36

it's a bloody bore because it's so elementary. It doesn't give you anything new. Your sense of completeness and balance comes out of your body. You have to coordinate in order to exist, so you demand this of a picture. If it doesn't correspond to a complexity of feelings that are a necessity to you, you don't care about it. The thing you look at will be of continuing interest to you if it makes a demand on you to respond. So it doesn't make any difference if the figures of the painting are geometric or human or vegetable. It's the totality of the picture, the figures and their environment in the picture, to which you respond.

A picture is just one of a multiplicity of things that people want, and in order to get them they make them. People want to make pictures and look at them and own them. It's one of the many things they do to express their enthusiasm for life.

? *And in so doing they must experiment?*

a A person doesn't experiment only in art. As he matures, his abilities demand that he understand more in every field. Why good cooking? You could survive on a woodchuck cooked over an open fire. Fortunately your curiosity will make you try different things with food. Curiosity is innate in man.

In my work, I am trying to communicate a visual statement of my interests and enthusiasms from day to day and year to year. The visual structure of the picture, the design of the picture, the color of the picture, all have a quality that is instantaneously apparent and creates the same mood in the spectator that the artist experienced in the process of doing it.

I am not painting for a definite audience. However, I know I'm working for an audience. I don't know who it is, but I know there are thousands of people responding to my work. It's clear that I wasn't making the picture for them, but their response means that they, in some sense, have responses to life that have some similarity to my own. It makes me feel good, this response. They don't think about it. They just like your work. When you're painting, you're not thinking about them. This doesn't mean I'm snooting the audience. I know it exists. If I find a picture satisfying, I know thousands of others will find it so. If there's something wrong with the picture, others will know it, too.

I simply take it for granted that art is of first importance as a value in life and that it has to be created in a sense of complete freedom. It gives value

Rapt at Rappaport's. Oil. The Joseph H. Hirshhorn Foundation

to your own capacities to perceive and feel. It's a
celebration of your faculties, your capacity to think
sensitively. I think art is very healthful, very
modest, and very important as a moral value.

By modest I mean that you're not pretending to
anything. You're just pleased with what you have,
your faculty to perceive what is worthwhile.

? *Your mother and father were both artists. Is this why
you became one?*

a Some people are born with an impulse to be artists—
people who have had no contact with art through their
families or otherwise. The same thing is true in music,
where somebody learns to play an instrument although

38

the family tries to discourage him, as was the case with
Leonard Bernstein. The indomitably creative person
has a compulsion that can't be stemmed. In my case,
I had the continuing drive to be an artist, as well as
the background. You have to want to create all the
time. Playing a musical instrument is hard, too, but
there's only one way to do it and that is to practice
continuously. The same thing applies to art. There's
no getting around it. Art is the product of the desire
of the person to paint. Picasso is a striking example.
He just makes pictures all the time, day and night,
seven days a week. Why does he do it? He can't help
himself.

? *Can you trace the evolution of your style?*

a An artist's style evolves by virtue of his training and
his personal preferences as time goes on. At a very
early stage of my art studies the 1913 Armory Show was
held. It was the first showing in the United States of
the most contemporary and advanced European art of
that time. I felt very fortunate to be able to see this
show. I also had five watercolors in it, and I sold
one, which was quite a feat. The names of the
European artists who are commonplace today were
virtually unknown then. All the work from Courbet
through the Impressionists and the Postimpressionists
and the Fauves and the emerging Cubists made a
tremendous impression on me. This work had never
been brought together, even in Europe. It was a
revelation, a world's fair of ideas, a complete
bombshell. It didn't repudiate anything I already
knew, but it opened up a whole panorama of
possibilities that had no counterpart in American art.
Today, of course, with all the communication available,
anything that goes on in the world is known everywhere
else in the world. Then, it was not the case. Even
Americans who went to Europe could not have
received this total impression of the then contemporary
art world to the degree the Armory Show presented it.
　　Before the Armory Show, I had attended the Henri
School, founded by Robert Henri. He was the leader
of a group of radical artists of the day known as "The
Eight." John Sloan, George Luks, and William
Glackens were also members. I'd worked in the manner
of the free realism of the Henri School, but, with the
Armory Show, my scope was suddenly expanded. The
Henri concept of art as being directly relevant to
contemporary life wasn't in any sense repudiated by
European modernists. They simply had a more

Semé. Oil. The Metropolitan Museum of Art,
George A. Hearn Fund, 1953

sophisticated vocabulary. Certainly if anybody leaned
on nature, it was Cézanne, and if anybody could be
called a realist, it was Courbet, and if anybody was
interested in light, it was the Impressionists—so the
direct relationship between nature and art was
explicit in modernism.

? *If you had to start over again, would you choose a
different kind of art training from that which you had?*

a God, I wouldn't want to start all over again. Training,
of course, is most important in art as well as in any

other line of human endeavor. Any training in painting that doesn't prevent you from developing your maximum potential is all to the good, whether it is a so-called academic approach or a loose-leaf, liberal attitude. I had the latter. The Henri School was different from the official art training of the day. Henri was opposed to the Academy. He accented the source of art as being based in life and not in rules that had been codified, giving the right way to draw and the right way to paint. So in his classes we drew from the model, and we drew outside the school in the streets, cafés, and so on. But the accent was on making a picture directly from your experience with life. You were not to turn out a standardized and approved picture in the style of the day.

The classic training, which taught the student to draw a head or a vase or bowl of fruit, is all to the good, on the principle that the more knowledge you have the better. But this doesn't automatically guarantee you'll make a good work of art.

I think drawing is all-important. It is impossible to use color without making some kind of a drawing. Drawing is simply the dividing up of a space. What you do with it is the important thing. If you take a sponge filled with red paint and throw it onto a canvas, you've made a drawing because you've divided up the space. But the division of space can be either meaningful or stupid, so that the place of drawing in art is primary at all times. Drawing is objectively necessary in order to communicate the subjective content of your experience. Drawing is, essentially, the constructing of an object. You are building something, giving your subjective experience a physical identity. Knowing this, you realize that you have to learn the rules of effective construction, which is drawing.

? *To what degree has the camera influenced art?*

a It is an extension of the sense of sight and gives it permanence and angles of vision that were not possible before. It hasn't changed the purpose of art in any sense, but it's made certain kinds of painting unnecessary. In the past there were a lot of realistic paintings done of scenes and people. Now you can take a camera on your vacation instead of having paintings made of what you see. It has affected painting in this sense—as a form of reporting. But it hasn't changed art and it hasn't changed people.

Nu. Oil. Collection of Ira Herbert. Courtesy of Downtown Gallery

? *What artists have been important to you personally?*

a In the beginning, Robert Henri and his group. I had
the advantage of my family's association with these
artists. I just took their attitude toward things for
granted and felt this was the way to be. But when I saw
the Europeans, I reacted very strongly. A Van Gogh
reproduction is in every hotel room today, but at that
time he was a complete surprise. Later I was influenced
by Seurat, Picasso, and Léger, among others.
I don't collect anything. I have no interest in

owning works of art. I don't have any of my own paintings around. I'm developing my ideas all the time, and the one I'm working on represents all of them. If I have the others around, they distract me. Now if you asked what artists interest me, that would be different. I think there is more art going on right now than in any other period of the human race,

Stuart Davis

including the Renaissance. Every newspaper, magazine, radio program has some reference to art. The amount of art being sought, produced, talked about is unprecedented. Because of the vast amount, there is a lot of bad art, but then there always was. There's a lot of good art, too.

? *Do you think an artist must have talent to succeed?*

a I think he's in a hell of a fix if he hasn't. Of course other factors are important to success. Endless energy, and some people have that. It's a talent in itself, and the more you have the better. Hard work, including self-criticism.

? *Can you visualize the finished painting immediately?*

a In a sense, yes, and yet the more you know, the more you don't know. Painting itself can open up ways to say things you couldn't say before. I always have the need to express moods and deeper feelings.

My first response to a subject is a spontaneous, unpredictable response to something—a nonanalytical, personal reaction of excitement and interest. Of course, something else has entered the situation already that causes you to formulate this subjective feeling in an objective visual vocabulary.

I couldn't have painted any other way than I did. It simply didn't interest me. I bought a book of Toulouse-Lautrec reproductions in 1912. In those days, not many people knew who he was. Now everybody does. Only in the last ten to fifteen years has the balance swung the other way, toward modern art. The dealers have promoted it, but it wouldn't work unless the public accepted it as corresponding to life. The tempo of life is not in academic work. Modern art has a contemporary feeling. I, along with some other people, was ahead of the time in recognizing it.

? *And now your taste has been justified. How does it feel to have people agree with you?*

43   **a** To me it feels quite natural.

5

ADOLF DEHN

**22 famous
painters
and
illustrators
tell how
they work**

Photograph of the artist

A vigorous artist, Adolf Dehn shows equal skill whether he is painting a documentary picture or sketching for his own amusement. One of the acknowledged greats among modern lithographers, Dehn enjoys working on stone but he has never lost his affection for other media. He has won two Guggenheim Fellowships (1939 and 1951). His work hangs in a score of museums, among them the Metropolitan Museum, the Whitney Museum, the Brooklyn Museum, the Museum of Modern Art, the Chicago Art Institute, and the Carnegie Institute. He has taken first prize at many art shows and exhibitions, among them the International Water Color Exhibition at the Chicago Art Institute in 1943 and the Philadelphia Print Club and Library of Congress shows. Born in Waterville, Minnesota, Dehn studied for three years at the Minneapolis School of Fine Arts. He also attended the Art Students League in New York City on a scholarship. He has taught at the Colorado Springs Fine Arts Center, and the Norton Museum School in Palm Beach, Florida. He exhibits regularly at the Milch Gallery in New York City. Dehn is a member of the National Academy, the American Water Color Society, the Society of American Graphic Artists, and the Century Association.

Versatility   I'm not like some artists who can't decide what to do. My own conflict is that I'm overwhelmed with too many things I'd like to paint. Color, composition, texture, subject matter, everything excites me.

? *How do you manage to communicate so much excitement in your work? You have great versatility, but your work is never technically cold and distant.*

a   I surely haven't sought versatility. I never did much thinking about it. I just worked the way I wanted to work. I would make nonrepresentational paintings today, but I'm not interested. I work at what I like.

? *Are you saying then that your career as an artist developed spontaneously, that you never consciously mastered any of your technical skills, that they just happened?*

a   Certainly not. Of course I worked hard to master those disciplines that any artist must possess. But the medium must excite me. For example, I worked in

The Dark One. Gouache.
Collection of the Whitney Museum of American Art, New York.
Gift of Mr. and Mrs. Albert Hackett

black and white entirely until 1936. From art-school
days, I had some kind of phobia about color. As a boy
growing up I copied Charles Dana Gibson and James
Montgomery Flagg. I copied them line for line in
black and white, and they were good copies.

I always felt more comfortable working in black and
white, and I had never painted with any ease or
assurance. So often people told me, "You're actually
painting in black and white," when they saw my
drawings and lithographs.

Finally, in 1936, I felt unbelievably frustrated.
I had dwelt upon this problem a great deal. I knew
I would have a greater satisfaction, and probably
greater success, if I mastered painting. When I came
back from Europe that year, I thought it out very
carefully. I decided that I was a lazy coward. I had
been making watercolors in black and white washes
for years. But I didn't have the courage to learn to
handle color. I decided to teach myself. I floundered
several days and then broke the ice. I'll tell you how
I did it. I knew a good deal about color, but
I couldn't put colors together so they worked easily.
Either it became a tinted sort of drawing or a mess of
unrelated color. This is how I solved the problem.
I set up a reproduction of a Marin watercolor and then
took a mountain scene I had drawn in Austria. I tried

to work in the manner of Marin and learned an enormous amount. As I worked, the color became an integral part of the design, and I realized I was painting at last—and it did not look like a Marin. I was so excited, I actually had tears in my eyes. I had broken the ice. I knew it. Then I put my experiments aside and started painting. I made many bad ones and some were good. My pleasure in the medium was boundless, and it soon led to a considerable success. I never had confidence in painting until 1936. It was gained only after experimentation and hard work.

Adolf Dehn

? *Can you tell us a little bit about your early days?*

a I grew up in Minnesota in a little country town. I just drew when I was a little boy the way little boys and girls draw. In adolescence, I had the usual excitement in sports, basketball, and girls, only I kept on drawing after the others stopped. I wanted to be an artist. I worked my way through Minneapolis Art School. In those days, we worked our way through. Summers I worked for carpenters, fished for the market on the hometown lake, did some church decorating to earn money, and took care of a furnace for my room when I was in art school. I was living on very little money and was always hungry. My family was poor. It didn't occur to me that they should help me.

My father was a trapper during the winter months. Summers he was a fisherman. He was a free agent. He had the temperament of an artist. He didn't want to knuckle under to a boss. We had a garden and a cow and chickens and even pigs. We lived off this.

My mother was a romantic and wanted me to be an artist. My father believed that I should do what I wished but warned me that it was a difficult career to follow. If I should be a failure, I was to remember that he had warned me. Luckily I did well enough so he could be quite proud of me. He was very good at bragging about his son.

? *Was your training at Minneapolis helpful in the long run?*

a Yes, to a degree. Well, they believed in tradition. It was the old atelier system. You had to draw from casts for the first year. A certain amount of anatomy is fine, but this was deadening. You had to draw an ear for a week. Then you did the eyes. Then the hand. Then the whole body. Drawing was taken seriously and that's fine, but they didn't know how to teach drawing. Copying isn't drawing. I love drawing. When

Sacred Ride. Casein

the eye, the heart, the brain, and the hand merge into a spontaneous gesture, you have drawing.

The training at the Minneapolis Art School must have been good in many ways for after the third year the Art Students League of New York awarded Wanda Gag and myself a scholarship. Nobody from the school had ever won one before. It would have been very embarrassing if one or the other of us had won it since we were going together at the time. Luckily we both won.

I had $32.10 in my pocket when I reached New York. To go to school it was necessary to find a job right away. I did after three weeks, with the Holmes Electric Protection Company as a night watchman. I worked nights and went to school during the day. I couldn't go to John Sloan's class at the League because it was held in the evening. However, I took a class with Kenneth Hayes Miller.

Miller was a formidable man. He asked me on my first day, "May I see some of your work? You're from Minneapolis? Forget Minneapolis." That was what Miller did for me. It was a negative thing. But his teaching eradicated the literal and academic approach.

At that time, the work of Boardman Robinson influenced me more than any other contemporary artist. He influenced many students such as Reginald

Marsh, Aaron Bohrod, and David Friedenthal. A friend who knew him said, "You go to him and tell him I sent you, he'll be nice to you." He was. His wife, Sally, would cook us a dinner. He would look at my sketches, make suggestions, and I was overwhelmed when he, the Master, would ask me to criticize his work.

Adolf Dehn

? *In those days you were supporting yourself with a variety of jobs, as well as commercial and fine art. Did this bother you?*

a Of course. The odd jobs were dull and paid badly. I thought I would try commercial art, but I hadn't the proper enthusiasm, so never succeeded, and in retrospect this delights me.

? *When did your works first appear?*

a When I was still in art school. *The Masses Magazine,* which was a rebellious periodical of poetry, literature, and art, was the first to reproduce a drawing of mine. Soon thereafter, *Playboy* and *Broom,* avant-garde magazines of the twenties, printed my drawings. *The Dial,* which is now considered to have been the finest literary magazine of the twenties, reproduced a great many of my things. One of the good aspects of *The Dial* was that they were able to pay for the work. Also Frank Crowninshield, editor of *Vanity Fair* magazine, was very kind and used many pages of my satirical drawings.

? *Did you gravitate to lithography because you liked the medium, or were you motivated by a trend of the time?*

a There was really no trend toward lithography at that time. It is true that George Bellows was then making some of his fine lithographs, also Arthur B. Davies and Albert Sterner were working on the stone. Boardman Robinson had made a few prints, and it was he who urged me to try lithography. It was a natural medium for me. I loved the hard chaste resistant stone, the subtle nuances, and the rich blacks that I discovered came spontaneously.

After having made several lithographs, I was fortunate to be invited to show two of the prints in the largest graphic exhibition of the year. Carl Zigrosser, the print expert, who was then with the Weyhe Gallery, after seeing my prints asked me to join his gallery. So without even thinking about it, I had a gallery. The first drawing he sold was

49

Central Park Night. Casein

purchased by Arthur B. Davies, who was considered
about the greatest American artist at that time. It
made me feel pretty good.

? *Your years in Europe had an important effect on your
work and your development as an artist. What made
you go in the first place?*

a Every young artist wanted to go to Europe. We wanted
to experience the European way of life—the art, the
architecture, the customs, and what we considered the
superior cultural attainments.

The problem of getting enough money together
seemed insurmountable. With some luck, a few sales
were made, and I took steerage on the old *Zeeland,*
about the oldest ship sailing on the Atlantic at that
time. John Singer Sargent was in first class—we didn't
meet.

As for the effects on my work and development as an
artist, there were many. Naturally I was impressed by
the old masters in the museums, but I was more
directly influenced by the contemporary artists of
France and Germany—such as Picasso, George Grosz,
and Pascin. The German Expressionists in general
excited me. I took some delight in Paul Klee and
Kandinsky. But quite as important an influence was
the European way of life—the ease, the leisure for
which I had a great talent, and which was possible
because during the Great Depression the American

50

dollar went a long way. For instance, the first six
months in Vienna, after having lived in New York on
a subsistence level, I found myself living in true
luxury on twenty-five dollars a month. To illustrate,
the best seats in the theater would cost ten cents, a
fine meal with a bottle of good wine cost fifteen
cents, my room with breakfast less than a dollar a
month.

**Adolf
Dehn**

    I lived in Europe and in the main, Vienna, seven
years.

? *Do you travel to get ideas for paintings or to absorb
the sensations of a different place, different people?
Are these impressions eventually translated into a
painting?*

a I never go any place just to get subject matter.
I want to see what's over the next hill, that's all.
I've been to Greece, for example, and that's a very
exciting place, but I've never done any paintings of
Greece. The first time I went to Italy, I didn't do
anything with that material. The second time I went,
a series of paintings were made from sketches.

    I think one should concentrate on whatever one sees
that pleases, that excites in nature. Or maybe it
will be certain types of human beings that are
exciting. One starts thinking in pictorial terms when
traveling in new places. You can't help asking
yourself, How would you work this out in terms of a
picture? If you're on the scene with a sketchbook,
you make notes. I make fewer notes now than I did.
I find that the less data I have the more freedom
I have in executing that which gets me going. I often
do better work after I've been away from a place that
excites me. When I'm closer to it, it's too literal.
Later, it's been strained through the sieve of time,
and the essence remains. Yet I don't work out of
memory entirely. I find I paint a picture and out of
that grows another picture and another and another.
They veer off and suddenly a "sport" appears—
something entirely different—I have an illegitimate
strain going.

? *Can you tell us more about your working methods?*

a There are those wonderful moments when you get up
in the morning and want to start working on a new
concept. You work feverishly without thinking, letting
it flow out of your hand. Sometimes such a picture is
finished in one session. More often it needs

51
considerable reworking and study. However, I feel

Tuscan Hills. Gouache

the need of working every day, and I force myself to go into the studio and try to work on earlier compositions if there happens to be no great excitement for a new painting.

? *Would you say that the nature of the predilections in your own work limit your enjoyment of other art?*

a It seems to me that my taste is catholic. Among contemporary paintings the whole range from the academic works of the realistic school to the, by now, academic work of the avant-garde school can be pleasurable and stimulating. From a technical point of view, the flamboyant dash of the better action painters offers a new boldness of approach. However, the great artists of the past are the real fountain of my inspiration today. When I think of Rembrandt and Goya and Daumier and Brueghel, Courbet, Manet, and the great Chinese, these action painters dwindle into gesticulating exhibitionists. I can't imagine these pictures will endure. There is no content. At best there is texture, color, and design. If they don't go back and get some of the things that Goya and Rembrandt had, they will wither on the vine.

? *Why is it Rembrandt everyone respects and mentions?*

a It seems to me it is because he feels more deeply the human being. God, it's just heartbreaking looking at some of those portraits. It's like looking at your father when he's ready to die. Rembrandt comes as close as anybody ever did to revealing the human experience. He had great technical equipment to do what he wanted to do. Thousands have had that, but they didn't have that great depth of feeling.

? *What would you say about the importance of talent and originality?*

Adolf Dehn

a There are professional painters who have little talent and originality. The same can be said for several million amateurs—however, there are a good many amateurs who do have these qualities. It seems to me talent is a facility, a capacity to do a thing well; originality is a way of seeing—feeling— that has a unique personal quality. The artist's work that possesses it stands out—is memorable.

Picasso is *the* example of originality. But he has stolen more ideas since the beginning of time than almost anybody. He's looked at everything. But his talents are so great, his powers are so great, it's still a Picasso. You don't say of Picasso, "too much African sculpture." He has created something uniquely his. If you can do that, you somehow give each finished work a new importance. He has also been stolen from more than any living artist or dead one. But thieves who steal from Picasso don't have his power of doing something different.

Many of the most talented young people do not succeed. They have the notion that sheer talent will carry them to achievement. Talent must be combined with enduring hard work. Laziness is often half-sister to talent, and to succeed she should be exterminated.

? *You have talked to many young artists over the years. What advice do you give them?*

a When parents of the very young come to me and say, Has my boy or girl enough talent? Should he take up art as a career? I say to the parents, "Even if the young person seemingly has talent, don't urge him to be an artist professionally. Do urge him to take it up as an avocation." Nobody should go into art as a profession unless the drive is so strong that he can't help himself.

It is a hard, often precarious life, but a wonderful one. I have never wanted to follow any other course.

6

STEVAN DOHANOS

**22 famous
painters
and
illustrators
tell how
they work**

Photograph of the artist

Stevan Dohanos is a passionate realist who finds
pleasure and beauty in the simplest forms of nature.
Gifted as an illustrator, he can endow the most
common objects with distinction. He has expressed his
talents in virtually every field of art. He is an
internationally known magazine cover artist, an
illustrator, a painter. He has designed four U.S.
postage stamps, handsome weathervanes, rugs, signs,
door knockers. His personally designed "Dohanos
Tabouret" can be found in artists' studios around
the world.

Born in the small Ohio steel town of Lorain,
Dohanos sold newspapers to augment the family
income. He took a home study course in art while he
was in high school, and later attended night classes at
an art school in Cleveland on a scholarship. This
training prepared him for a job as an apprentice in a
Cleveland art studio. After six years there he moved to
New York City, where in a few short years he became
one of the best-known illustrators in America.

Victimized twice by tuberculosis, Dohanos has given
generously of his time to the National Tuberculosis
Association, designing seals for their campaigns. He
has also designed posters and seals for the Red Cross,
the Community Chest, the U.S. Government, and
dozens of civic causes in his adopted home town of
Westport, Connecticut.

Dohanos has served twice as President of the Society
of Illustrators and is a member of the American Water
Color Society.

Realism

I feel that any serious artist or writer collects a
wheelbarrow full of research material before he begins
work. You might just use a few square inches of that
wheelbarrow load, but in this extensive research, you
will find something that is so wonderful you'll create
a terrific picture. Once you discover the rewards of
intensive research, you will know without question
that it's a procedure that pays off. You'll know then
that there are no shortcuts in developing a good
picture. In my own case, I think my carefulness
probably comes out of my own personal background.
I grew up in rather lean circumstances, and I had no
great confidence. I had to earn my way in life.
Everything I did, I had to do very carefully. I had
to keep my jobs. When I delivered work, I wanted it
researched and carefully done. I was an obedient kind
of worker and anxious to please, very anxious to

Shoppers' Festival, Yokohama, Japan. Water color

please. You want to be right. It's an embarrassment, let's say, to be told something is wrong in your painting. You can explain it, but it gives you a feeling that you've let the job down.

? *Doesn't the kind of exacting research you do take a good deal of time?*

a Yes, it does take time to document a picture thoroughly, but I think it is time well spent. One of the things I prided myself on when I first hit the art market in New York and was beginning to be established was my interest in research. I had a passion for realism and naturalism, and this compelled me to bring to my client complete information in my pictures. This was, I believe, a contribution. In most

**Stevan
Dohanos**

advertising and story illustration of that period,
there wasn't this interest in detail. Some of my
first illustrations were noticed because they were
very carefully documented. I would spend several days
and sometimes months checking out a subject. When
the *Saturday Evening Post* gave me my first assignment
it was a story about the South Seas, a six-part serial.
I had never been to that part of the world, so my
first challenge was to decide what I would paint.
I went to every possible source of information, the
libraries and museums. I telephoned people and
begged and borrowed every bit of information before
I planned the picture. Later, a native of that area told
me, "I was convinced you had been to Tahiti. You
couldn't have faked those pictures."

? *I can understand why such meticulous research is
necessary for an assignment like this, but why do you
spend so much time studying common, ordinary
objects that surely must be familiar to you?*

a We take for granted the so-called common object. For
example, you think you know what a fire hydrant looks
like, but a true artist will find out that there are,
maybe, twelve different styles of hydrants, and he
must pick the one that is absolutely right for his
picture. Or maybe you want to use an awning in a
picture. Awnings can be endlessly different in design
and structure. Obviously you shouldn't settle for an
image you have in your mind of an awning. Through
legwork or professionally motivated curiosity, you
will unearth tremendous variations, artistic
possibilities, in colors and shapes of awnings. It's
detail I know, but when you multiply that research by
everything in your painting, you surround yourself
with limitless possibilities. So you think you know
everything about awnings? There's a bar that comes
down. What else? In the process of researching this
everyday object, I run a few awnings up and down.
I ask questions of shopowners. "Why is the awning up
today?" "What time of year do you put them away?"
I've unlocked my mind, and the first thing I know I've
not only solved the problem of this painting, but I've
gotten ideas for several more. It may be
time-consuming, but it's standard procedure for me,
par for the course. I've seen artists who aren't willing
to spend money to make money. They say, I won't
have to rent this chair or buy those photographs or
travel a bit to research a picture. This is shortsighted.
What you invest in a picture compounds its interest.

Time Was. Tempera on wood

? *You never feel that so much research and attention to detail slows you down, destroys your spontaneity as an artist?*

a I've sometimes wondered about this danger of having so much documentation that you become waterlogged with information. It can get in the way of spontaneity. But I get that spontaneity out of my system when I go out and knock off a nice painting of an old house.

? *Would you say that your paintings are quite literal renderings of the reality you see as a human being?*

a You mean, why am I so slavish to nature and the subject? Because I believe so in the things I am painting that I don't like to tamper with or alter what has inspired me. I spend weeks, say, finding the right person for a picture. When I do paint him,

I don't want to make his neck longer to make him stylish. I want to paint him the way he is. I cast him very carefully, and that's the way I want to paint him.

? *Then you must have a concept of the picture you are going to paint before you go out and begin "casting." Do you pick your characters or realistic objects to fit a picture you see in your imagination?*

Stevan Dohanos

a I have a concept, and then I let the pieces come together. I like to let the picture design itself. I'm just the intermediary. I am not bound by the picture in my head. Imposing your clichés and inventions on yourself is apt to keep you from going out to see the subject. When you do go out to see the subject, it suggests so many believable truths. You think you could sit down and draw a tree in your studio. You begin a few sketches. There is something unsatisfying about it. Then you go out and look, and you see something you have never thought of. Perhaps it is the twist of the branches, the limbs, that is so artistically beautiful.

? *Where do you get your ideas for pictures?*

a My ideas are rooted in my experience. I am very impressed by environment. My surroundings are my inspiration. Because I was born in a small town, these impressions stay with me. My environment and background have made me a thoughtful observer of life. I have an appreciation of what's real, the sober responsibility of life, of how most people live day by day. I've said this often, but I'll say it again. I see beauty in the commonplace. How did this begin? I grew up in a factory-town environment in Ohio. We weren't conscious of man-made fashion and style and beauty. I didn't come up through the graceful process of art schools and European trips and other nice things that have influenced other artists. In my home town, there was no great opportunity to have aesthetic experiences. I stumbled along through a home study course in art, encouraged by my friends. Then I went to a very hard-working commercial art studio where we turned out a pretty nuts-and-bolts kind of product. The thing that saved me was that several people in my home town saw my potential when I was copying and sketching things. That was the break that made an artist out of me. I was just interested in a well-paying job of any kind. I thought

Cover illustration. Tempera.
Reprinted by special permission of *The Saturday Evening Post.*
© 1951 The Curtis Publishing Company

I had it made when I became a railroad clerk. If you
had a white-collar job, you were something. Just about
the time I was getting some place in the job, I decided
to transfer to the art studio. To my parents, it was
the unknown against the sure thing, but in six years,
I had become what they called "a top studio man."
That was the farm league—out there in Ohio. When
I was ready for the big league, a studio man from New
York came out and found me.

? *How did you develop your personal style if you were
doing nuts-and-bolts stuff to order in the art studio
where you were working?*

Stevan Dohanos

a A chink of light appeared that illuminated my rather limited background. I suddenly awoke to the fact that there was a gallery world. I visited my first art gallery in Cleveland and started to tamper with painting just a bit while I was working in the studio. I went to a few sketch classes, and I got stung. We would go out along the railroad tracks where factory workers lived. I took to sketching right away, and I never got over it. Through a little guidance from Frank Wilcox of the Cleveland School of Art, I moved along. These were my first original paintings. Before that, I was just copying. I could render and work hard, but as far as doing anything original went, I just hadn't tried it up until that point. I wasn't capable of a pretty, pretty kind of art. I never had the flair for that. The chic and the stylish just didn't come across to me. But when I had a little success painting the kind of scene I liked and the people I knew, I realized that this was mine.

? *Were you consciously developing a style of your own, or did it naturally evolve?*

a I suppose it was natural at first, and then when I saw what direction I was taking, I worked at my kind of approach, my kind of subject. The point is to develop something that can be yours and salable. You want them to come to you, and then you can run with it. After I got to New York, it took several years of regrouping to develop that style. When you have something of your own, you have reached the first plateau of success. This starts the cash register ringing. It isn't easy to develop an original style. You have to do it through observation and checking other people. In other words, if you know that something is being covered by several other people, you just cross it off your list. People associate a certain kind of art with me. That's what builds up a prestige and an image for an artist. It's possible for any artist to develop a personal style.

? *When did this style of yours begin to crystallize? When did you receive public recognition for it?*

a In the 1930's, I got a fortunate assignment in the Virgin Islands. Five artists were sent by the United States government to paint anything they liked in the Islands. I was one of them. When I got there, in spite of the well-known tropical beauty of the place, I found myself looking for the same homey, environmental thing I liked to paint at home.

61

Cover, Annual Report. Tempera on canvas.
Standard Oil Company, Inc., in New Jersey

I prowled around the shacks and talked to the mothers.
I painted the backyards, the women cooking, the
laundry hanging out. I didn't paint the façade of the
place—the harbor, the people in the streets. One
government official said, "You can trust Steve to
always find the small human thing to paint."

This trip made me known as "the guy who catches
the spirit of the tropics." I began to get advertising
assignments and then the *Saturday Evening Post*
noticed me. They asked me to illustrate a Nordhoff
and Hall serial. Later when I submitted a group of
cover ideas to them I hit it with the American *genre*
thing. The steady flow of these paintings went on for
fifteen years. They wrapped up in a single picture this
particular artist's passion and concentration on the
documentary. I like what one citation said of me. It
called me "an interpreter of the American scene."

? *You have no fear of the simple idea then? If a subject appeals to you emotionally, you want to paint it?*

Stevan Dohanos

a When I'm going out to look for an idea, I don't pick the pretty dress or the pretty face. I don't feel this is going to help me sell the thing I have faith in. The medium level of truth is a much safer thing to work in. We all laugh when we come out of a movie full of action and adventure and the girl's dress is never torn and her hair isn't mussed. I like realism, and I like to paint real objects.

? *Like that loaf of bread, that still life on the wall?*

a Yes. When I saw this loaf of bread, I knew I would paint it for its nuances, the cracks, the shades of brown. It was twenty inches wide when I put it under my arm. I felt I had a friend! The weight of that loaf stayed with me throughout the painting. I did this picture in France. I used to prowl the Paris market and try to decide what to paint. In such a market, you had the prettiest delicacies. But what kept catching my eye was the wheels of cheese and the bread. This picture could be used editorially. It could be a poster or used to illustrate an advertisement. I like to think that in this picture I have not just painted a still life but that the picture reaches much farther. Bread is the staff of life. It expresses to me the pleasure and necessity of living. It's not a fancy bakeshop bread. It's a peasant loaf. It makes you think of bread and hunger and how some people have too much food and others not enough. It appeals to the sensory nerves. It reminds you of the Bible. It starts a chain of thinking. I've edited the picture down to its essential meaning by choosing a loaf with a certain shape, using a strong knife, putting it on a well-worn baker's board and suggesting sackcloth for the background.

? *How important is this editing?*

a I edit constantly. The final product may seem ordinary and realistic, but there's been a continual process of editing and designing throughout the period of preparing the picture. I think this kind of preparation is all-important for anyone who wants to do a still life. If you like to paint still life and you're good at it, then try to arrange objects that are homogeneous in theme. Your still life might suggest the sea or science or primitive objects, but it should say something. Don't just take a vase, a knife, a flower. You haven't said anything. You've only said you can paint well. A lot of painters, amateur and professional, paint a still life simply as shapes and related colors. They arrange objects that have no real related meaning when grouped together.

Stevan Dohanos

? *What are you trying to say to the people who look at your pictures?*

a I want people to see their environment. The people who move around in their environment have stopped seeing it. They aren't aware of what's around them. The trained artist can stop the clock so to speak. His eye can pick up something that's routine but that has gone unnoticed. If I go to a commencement ceremony, I don't just sit there like a fulfilled parent. My professional nerve ends are reminding me that there is a little group of people sitting over there who might make a picture. The light strikes them in a very dramatic way. Of course, there are periods when I'm tired or lazy. I may pass up my prerogative to be an observer. But most of the time my mind is alert and on the prowl.

? *I gather this is a pleasure?*

a It's a limbering exercise, a way to keep in trim. I am also fascinated with people. I like to tell the story of people without necessarily painting them. Each person surrounds himself with manners and habits, and these are very revealing. When you visit someone in a hospital, his room may be very neat while the next person's is all confusion. This is very meaningful to the artist. It reveals character. Luckily my eye is drawn to little bits of action, things people do. Out of their physical behavior you can easily get a visual portrayal of their character.

? *Do you use a camera when you are making notes in the field?*

a I do. I also make written notes, borrow swatches of clothing, anything that helps me record my impression of a scene. The camera is an aid, and any thinking artist will use it. If Da Vinci had owned one, he would have used it. In my case, the photograph is just one more thing you work with. You should use it as a source of information and not as a foundation for your painting. Your goal is to create an individual

64

painting. You can tell a mile away the artist who has become a slave to the camera. That sticks out all over. A painter can go around a figure with a sketch, but the camera can only pick up one plane.

? *What is your procedure when you go out sketching, the first step in making a picture?*

a When I go out to sketch a barn, say, I think of how many people have painted red barns. I ask myself, do I want to paint another? If I do decide I want to, how can my barn be different? The very fact that I know I am facing a hazard is helpful. I may decide to walk away from the subject. That is the first and simplest thing to do. But if I am in good form, I may tackle it by saying to myself, "Let's see if I can make one more red barn come off." You're conscious of being different and of not following the mob.

? *I gather that you believe application is as important as talent in achieving success as an artist.*

a I'm a very stubborn hard worker. Right or wrong, I plow ahead. Nothing is too small to be overlooked. No effort is spared. It's just darned hard work. It's complete application at all times. I have always discounted the fact that I may have talent. I attribute the success I've had to a willingness to learn a skill. The other thing that is important is the personality of the artist, what he sees in life and what he wants to say. You have to have an intense desire to make your skills add up to something. By a twist of fate, I became an artist. I could have been something else, but I couldn't be anything but a creative person.

? *Isn't taste important in the field of illustration? Can it be acquired or developed if the artist's early background was limited?*

a Taste, like talent, is always growing in the person who makes the effort. You develop new techniques. New mediums are available. By traveling, exposing yourself to new ideas, your taste changes and develops. I was always willing to learn and listen and be shown, and throughout these thirty-five years I have been exposed to people who painted well and designed good things. I picked it all up. Your senses become sharpened. Taste is important. In this field, good taste is the yeast in the bread.

65

7

ALBERT DORNE

**22 famous
painters
and
illustrators
tell how
they work**

Photograph of the artist

Albert Dorne's career as a successful illustrator has seldom been equaled. During the 1930's and '40's he became the highest paid and most sought-after advertising artist in the country. Despite the many demands on his time and energy, however, Dorne never failed to help the young artists who came to him for advice. He counseled them, put them in touch with art directors and editors, and gave them the benefit of his long and hard-won experience as a professional. His interest in aspiring artists led to the creation of the Famous Artists Schools in 1947. As a self-taught illustrator who had mastered the craft of art on his own, Dorne knew at first hand what the beginning artist must learn. He practiced drawing every free moment he had; later his drive and discipline paid off. When he began working for advertising and editorial accounts, the assignments flowed in and they have never stopped. Today, however, the Famous Artists Schools come first. Wholly absorbed in teaching Dorne devotes himself to the Schools he founded, and in serving the profession he loves. Albert Dorne is a Past President of the Society of Illustrators and co-founder of the Code of Ethics and Fair Practices of the Profession of Commercial Art and Illustration. He has had more than ten one-man shows of his illustrations. In 1953 he was the first artist to be awarded a Gold Medal for "a distinguished career" by the New York Art Directors Club. In the year 1963 he received the Horatio Alger Award for Achievement from the American Schools and Colleges Association, Inc. He holds an honorary Doctor of Fine Arts degree from Adelphi College.

The Making of a 'Pro'

To me, drawing is the most important consideration in making pictures. Unless you know how to draw, you won't know the security of being able to express yourself clearly and fluently as an artist. I am not speaking primarily of the academic concept of figure drawing, how the "perfect" hand, for example, is constructed, but rather the structure or "architecture" of picture making. It is also the art of observation and communication. It includes knowing the principles of form, composition, value, line. Being able to draw is as essential to the artist as the craft of writing is essential to the writer.

If you are able to draw, you can devote yourself to saying what you think and feel. The more you know

The Salesman. Colored ink.
Courtesy of John Hancock Mutual Life Insurance Company

about drawing, the more productively creative you can
be. You are no longer concerned with "how" to draw,
but rather with "what" to draw. You are only
concerned with art, and your knowledge and skill in
the craft of drawing thus become the natural working
extension of your artistic and creative self.

? *It is up to you, then, to decide what to say—rather
than be concerned with how to say it?*

a That's right. If you have mastered the craft of
drawing, you are headed in the direction of making
good pictures. The great Ingres made a statement that
has always impressed me. He said, "Drawing is the
probity of art." When you are drawing, your real self
comes out. You can teach people about art, how to
draw and paint. You can teach them the principles
and aesthetics; you can teach what "art" is; you can
stimulate talent. But *art* in the final analysis can
be defined as what the individual as an artist does
with his knowledge and skill. Art is the reflection
of the personality of the creator.

Take Picasso's work. Whether his paintings are good or bad, there's never any question about who did them, the personality of this great artist is so powerfully reflected in his work.

Albert
Dorne

? *One of the striking things about Picasso's work, and which has, indeed, been noted by many art critics, is the way he breaks the rules. He is considered a very fine draftsman by traditional standards, and yet most of his paintings look to the uninitiated as if they had been crudely done and without knowledge. Could you comment on this?*

a He *is* a superb draftsman, and this knowledge and security of his craft enables him to depart from conventional rules—to experiment as he has done in an incredible variety of directions. Most great modern artists have done the same thing. Cézanne is a good example. Consider, for a moment, his "Boy in the Red Vest." There is a story about that picture that illustrates what I have been saying. Two men were looking at the picture and one said, "Isn't that an awfully long arm?" The other replied, "Yes, it is, but what a wonderful arm!"

Being able to draw gives you the confidence to express yourself. It gives you the artistic security to exaggerate, to try something different and unique. It gives you much latitude to be creative, to interpret in your own way, to take all sorts of liberties with nature and ideas, and when you are finished, to be essentially right—to know your picture has a sound fundamental structure.

? *How did you develop your own sure touch as a draftsman? You didn't go to art school.*

a I began to draw when I was about five years old. Later, as a New York City kid, I had the most wonderful break a boy could have had. I discovered the Metropolitan Museum of Art. We lived within roller-skating distance of the museum and I haunted the place from the time I was ten years old. I drew most of the sculpture and pieces of armor in the museum. I even copied the figures on the Grecian urns. I played hooky from school and would go to the museum every Monday and Friday for over two years. I found out later that my teachers knew about it all the time and condoned it. Actually, I'm sure I was the youngest person ever to be given a sketching permit by the museum. In addition to giving me so many

Country Store. Colored ink. *Collier's*

wonderful subjects to draw, the Met had a profound
effect upon me. I was able—in this marvelous
environment—to saturate myself with great art of all
ages. It affected me for the rest of my life. It taught
me to distinguish between the mediocre and the good.
Those early years in the Met shaped my values in art.

? *You still spend time in the museums and collect fine
art, don't you?*

a Every chance I get—and everywhere I go. I love
art—all art—contemporary and traditional alike.
I make no distinctions other than what, in my

opinion, is their quality as art. And I buy as much as
I can afford—and usually more!

? *Despite your early, and continuing interest in fine
art, you decided to become an illustrator. Was it
because you were a poor boy, and illustration offered
a way toward a satisfying and lucrative career?*

Albert
Dorne

a That was part of the reason. But another reason was
equally important to me. The fact that the
illustrator's work reached the public impressed me.
His pictures were printed. You had to go to a museum
to see the work of the painters. The beautiful art
books we have now, which bring fine reproductions of
paintings into the lives of millions of people, did not
exist then. Anyone, however, could open up the
Saturday Evening Post, Cosmopolitan, or most
magazines, and see the work of the best illustrators.
   I had read somewhere that some of these illustrators
received as much as thousands of dollars for pictures—
and that did it. I was going to be a commercial artist
and illustrator!

? *Did your family object, or did they encourage you to
seek a career in art?*

a My mother thought I was a genius—naturally! She
was, after all, my mother, and she encouraged me. She
knew how serious I was about becoming an artist,
because I had, in fact, decided to be one at an
unusually early age. I had pneumonia when I was five
and almost died. The doctor told my mother that if
I survived the crisis and the fever broke, I would
probably ask for something. (This was supposed to
mean I was interested in living.) He advised her to
give me whatever it was if she could. I did survive
the crisis. The morning after the fever broke, my
mother asked me if I wanted anything. All my life
I vividly remember saying (and I can give you no
reason for this), "I want paper and paints. I'm going
to be a famous artist and make a lot of money."

? *And you moved straight toward your goal?*

a No. I had some interruptions at the beginning. I had
to make money to support my mother and my brother
and two sisters. I was the oldest. I left school at
thirteen and sold newspapers, and then I became an
office boy and had a combination of other odd jobs.
I was always pretty good at making a living. But to be

Four Broadway Characters. Colored ink. *Collier's*

an artist was the motivating force of my life. At the age of seventeen, I decided to make the break and get started at becoming a commercial artist. I went to a man who ran a one-man art studio and offered to work for nothing as an office boy while I learned the business. The "nothing" as a salary sounded fine to him. But I still had to take care of my mother—and by this time I was also married so I had two families to support. I worked in the studio six days a week from nine to six-thirty. Then I'd get home, have supper and a nap, and go back to work all night seven nights a week from midnight to eight in the morning as a shipping clerk for a film company. I did this for a whole year. Finally, the artist I was working for founded a partnership, and I was made a full-fledged artist with a salary. I was able to give up my night job. After almost a year of this, I decided I could make more money—and perhaps find better work—as a free-lance artist. So I went out on my own.

Albert Dorne

? *Even though you worked hard and managed a back-breaking schedule it doesn't sound as though you had much of a struggle becoming an artist. Did you?*

a Yes I did. You always struggle. I can't, of course, take credit for whatever talent I had, but I did work hard and long. The only real struggle I had was trying to make better drawings. I was a hustler—I didn't have too much trouble getting work—and I worked every single day and night, including weekends. I worked because it was a compulsive need.

? *You say you hustled. Is it true you can't wait for somebody to call you in the art business, that you must continually show potential clients what you can do for them, even if this means constantly making the rounds?*

a Yes. You can't sit around and wait for the work to come to you. You have to make up your mind that you're going to show your work. An important part of being a commercial artist is selling yourself. You have to show the art buyer and the art director that you are not only a good artist but an intelligent guy as well, one who can make pictures that will interpret the ideas of the client—whatever they may be.

? *Are you saying, in effect, that the artist must be flexible and able to compromise if the job requires it? Don't clients want the individual approach and style that each artist can contribute?*

a Of course, they want the very best you can give as an artist, but it is equally important for you to give them what they need as advertisers. Commercial illustration—no matter how creatively artistic and skillful—is a business, and you have to understand why you are being hired to do a given picture. The success of any picture—no matter how beautifully done—depends upon whether its function is realized.

? *You are speaking now about illustration, not fine art? There is a difference?*

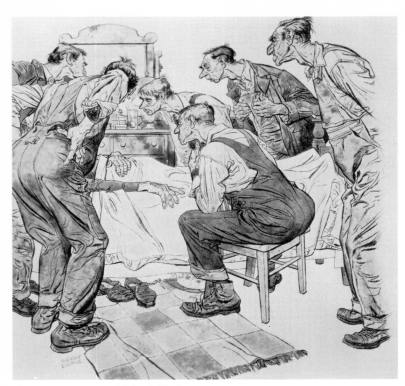

The Vultures. Colored ink. *Collier's*

a Certainly, there is a big difference. The difference
can be defined in terms of their ultimate use, the
reason for their existence. Commercial art is created
to move goods or to communicate ideas. It is, no
matter how creative, still an objective art produced
to convey the ideas of others. The painter, on the
other hand, can afford to express subjectively his own
feelings and his individual point of view. You accept
his art as a thing that exists for itself. It has a
life of its own. I deeply believe in the inherent
right of the painter to paint what he wants to paint.
However, the minute he takes on a specific
commitment for money, he has a responsibility to his
patron. I have great respect for the painter who will
work at unrelated jobs to support his family rather
than compromise with his convictions and his art. But
I firmly believe that the commercial artist must
function to fulfill the requirements of the client
74   who hired him.

? *Have you ever painted what you wanted to paint—for your own pleasure, so to speak?*

Albert Dorne

a I have never felt a need to make pictures for my own so-called pleasure. In the forty years I have been a professional artist, I have poured all my creative needs and expression into what I have done as an illustrator. Just let a client bring a problem, and I am challenged to find the most creative and artistic way to solve it. I have often compromised my point of view to solve a communications problem, but I have never compromised my art itself. For good or bad, it was always the very best I could do as an artist.

? *As a real professional who is proud of being one, can you give me your definition of the term "pro"?*

a "Pro" can be defined as an *attitude* more than anything else. I think a pro is a person who has tremendous respect for what he's doing and who never settles for anything less than the best of his capabilities. A real pro has a total devotion to what he does. He has an emotional and physical need to create and achieve the ultimate. He is a man of conviction who has a carefully nurtured image of perfect performance.

Ben Shahn once made a statement that explains how I feel. People are always asking him why he does commercial work. He says, "I'm proud to do this work. The only thing that is important to me is my attitude toward it. No matter what its ultimate use is *I am an artist at work*. I have the attitude of an artist whether I am doing a commercial assignment or painting a picture as my own personal expression."

I think the sweetest compliment any artist can get is to be called a pro.

? *Can you say anything for the amateur? Many people want to paint or draw for their own pleasure.*

a The amateur painter can also be a pro in attitude. The amateur who wants to be good must learn the basic steps in making a picture just as the professional must. He should make the same demands on himself. He should strive to do his best. Of course, he must learn to draw, to develop a respect for the architecture of pictures. All of this training is the basis of good picture making. Anyone, professional or amateur, who wants to know what he's doing in art must be well trained. After all, somebody had to teach a genius like Heifetz to play the fiddle and another like

Albert
Dorne

Rubenstein to play the piano. Knowledge and craft are what you must—and can—acquire whatever your ultimate purpose in making pictures. An artist must know what he is doing. You can be inspired and moved emotionally, but you still have to translate these emotions with deliberation and knowledge and skill onto a two-dimensional surface so that you can communicate these emotions to others.

? *What is the most significant change in illustration you have observed during the last thirty years?*

a I think it has been the gradual movement toward a marriage between illustration and fine art. The illustrator has more consciously tried to get more of the quality of fine art in his work. There is more imagination in illustration, more art, more spirit.

? *Isn't this fine-art influence partly a reaction to photography? Doesn't the illustrator have to compete with the photographer today?*

a Yes. He has to produce something photography can't give. He adds these things that set him apart—color, texture, personal style, and original techniques. *But you can't just do it merely with techniques or clichés or gimmicks or mannerisms.* The artist who develops an interesting new technique or original point of view must still come up with real content in his pictures.
  There is considerable pressure to innovate in the field of commercial art. The trouble is that many young illustrators think that technical innovation alone is what will make good art or make them a reputation. You have to have more than that. You have to say something to the audience.

? *Do you think the public is eager for innovation?*

a The public will accept and respond to innovation in art. There are, of course, no absolutes in art. The public taste is always changing and has changed several times since I began as an illustrator. The public today has been exposed to much more fine art and art philosophies, styles, and techniques than ever before through the incredible amount of beautiful art reproductions and art books as well as countless articles on art in our national magazines.

? *Are selectivity and emphasis essential to a good picture?*

a It is most important for the artist to know what to leave out and what to put in. This goes beyond craft.

This is the aesthetics of fine art, this business of selectivity.

? *What do you predict for the future of commercial art?*

a The future of commercial art is going to be a very good one for the good craftsman and the sound creative artist. Markets have diminished a little for the "upper crust" illustrator in national magazines, but they have grown a lot at the local level. There is great need for well-trained artists on the local level all over America. There is a scarcity of fine craftsmen, good all-around and creative artists as well as specialists who can do a good job.

? *What is the greatest satisfaction you get out of making a picture?*

a The most important thing to me is the *act* of making the picture—the experience of putting it together and seeing something come to life through my own efforts. I love the experience of drawing and painting and creating. After I finish a picture, however, I have no more interest in it. Over the years I gave them all away. I don't have a single one of my own paintings at my home or in my studio.

I collect other artists' work and enjoy the work of others. For me—because these pictures were done by someone else—they are an end in themselves. When I make a picture myself, the *end* is the doing of it.

? *You love teaching as much as painting, don't you?*

a I get enormous creative fulfillment out of teaching. I get a wonderful feedback from our students. I think it's a natural thing to want to teach. It's human nature. Having achieved some measure of fulfillment, the artist wants to pass it on. I think it's most human. That's why you find so many successful businessmen and lawyers, doctors, and others who devote a great deal of time to teaching.

I enjoy teaching. It's another impulse of fatherhood, I suppose, a sharing, a passing on. But a kind of selfishness is also involved here. Teaching satisfies the ego. It offers a kind of immortality.

I think all of the artists in this book teach for the same reason I do. It makes you feel a little taller, having helped someone.

8

ROBERT FAWCETT

**22 famous
painters
and
illustrators
tell how
they work**

Photograph of the artist

Known to many as the "illustrator's illustrator," Robert Fawcett has spent thirty-odd years earning the right to that title. A flawless draftsman, Fawcett received his early training at the Slade School of London University. There he drew continually, morning and afternoon, for two years.

Fawcett was born in the suburbs of London, but he grew up in Canada and New York City. His father, an amateur artist, wanted his son to paint and encouraged him to make a career of art. After receiving his training at the Slade, Fawcett returned to New York to establish himself as a commercial artist. He sold work almost immediately to leading magazines and today he is one of the top-ranking illustrators in editorial and advertising art. During the last decade, however, he has restricted his output of commercial work. In 1960 he was asked to paint a series of murals for the Commonwealth Institute of London, an assignment he found particularly congenial. At his studio-home in Ridgefield, Connecticut, Fawcett continues to explore his first love, pure drawing. His book *On the Art of Drawing*, expresses the consuming interest he has in this most basic element of art. He has won countless art directors' medals and awards.

Drawing

I was always drawing. I would draw my sisters, for example. I believe that if we can record the visual aspects of the world around us, we can go into deeper things. Like playing scales, it's got to be done. You may not like it, but it's got to be done. I compare this kind of art discipline to calisthenics. The athlete trains and trains and becomes stronger and more agile than he may ever need to be. But he's got to have this strength.

I would like people to see a sense of positive organization in my picture. If you see a picture that is well organized, you have no trouble looking at it. This is the logical outcome of drawing. Drawing is seeing. And what we do is create a kind of order in a picture that makes it easy for people to look at.

Michelangelo once said: "Drawing constitutes the fountainhead and substance of painting and sculpture and architecture. . . . Let him who has attained the possession of this be assured that he possesses a great treasure . . ."

I like to draw some things better than others. Nobody would ever ask me to do a he-she picture. They want me to do battle scenes and pictures with,

Oxford, Mississippi. Black and blue ink. *Look,* December 31, 1962

say, a Colonial background. This isn't bad. Besides, I don't happen to be interested in doing teen-age love scenes.

? *Did your early art training influence your taste for doing a certain kind of picture in a quality manner? Did it raise your standards?*

a Yes. I went to the Slade, the art school of London University. It was a period of strict discipline for me and a time when I was exposed to a cultural life I had never known. It was the finest school for draftsmen then—Augustus John was there. And they gave us discipline, discipline, discipline. One either gives in to it or rebels. Discipline was there, and I have never regretted that training.

? *Weren't you also influenced by the commercial world at that time?*

Robert Fawcett

a I started working in commercial studios when I was fourteen so I could save up enough money to pay for my first year at the Slade. Then by that time my father was doing a little better, and he helped me a bit with the second year.

I was always fascinated by art. From the age of seven, there was no doubt in my mind what I was going to do. Besides, if I'd tried to revolt my father would have got sore and probably whipped me, or something. I had no alternative. My father was a frustrated artist. He forced me into art, which is kind of unique. When I was seven he used to pay me to bring him drawings, and he'd give me a penny for them. Later when I was in grade school, he became a kind of art director and would bring work home for me to do. He had a built-in free-lancer. But I made him pay for them. Art represented a chance to get out of poverty. The illustrator's life seemed most desirable. A man like Charles Dana Gibson in those days was a public figure. I was influenced most by Howard Pyle. And then I used to copy stuff out of comic magazines as a boy. I must say I still see a little influence of this in my work.

? *Much of your book,* On the Art of Drawing, *has to do with the art of seeing. Why does the trained artist see things one way and the untrained person another?*

a Seeing is, after all, a relative thing, a personal thing. I'm just a built-in eye. I can see with such clarity. But the hand always falters between the eye and the paper. You and I *do* see the same thing. But if we start to record what we see, we will record different things. If I have a trained eye, I will record a more comprehensive picture because I know how to translate what I see. There should be the least amount of interference between the eye, the brain, and the hand. When you have exhautsed conventional seeing, you can go into the more interesting things.

It is very difficult to see without putting artificial barriers in front of you. The tendency is to see the conventional thing. You should always look at something as if you had never seen it before. After a period of penetrating observation, the same subject

The Cleric in Holmes' Room. Mixed media. *Collier's*

can begin to take on different aspects. This is what
I have described as "becoming dizzy with looking."

? *Do you ever spend considerable energy and time on a
subject and then decide it isn't really worth
painting?*

a Even an experienced artist sometimes makes mistakes.
It happened to me in Europe. I was making a lot of
drawings as we traveled through. I'd stop the car and
think, that's terrific. But after working fifteen
minutes, I'd find it wasn't a legitimate subject.
I would be drawn to it for its picturesque quality. But
when I started doing it, I had to decide this wasn't
for me. Nobody should force himself to draw
something that doesn't work. This is not discipline.
You should have fun drawing.

? *Do you think artists are born?*

a I do not. Neither do I think an engineer is born.
People are prone to put much too much emphasis on

natural talent. A career is a long time. I am less interested in what a child turns out at fifteen than I am in what that same person turns out at fifty. Sweat and application will develop the artist. An artist who wants badly enough to do it will do it anyway. It will be impossible to dissuade him. If students want to be spoon-fed, there is not likely to be a real desire on their part to be artists, but merely a whim. They must pursue constant and relentless drawing. Being able to draw only comes about by drawing. Of course, training will give an artist hints. But in the last analysis the artist develops himself.

Robert Fawcett

? *Is there always one "best" way to approach a subject and start painting?*

a There is one piece of advice that will work for everybody. This is an individual matter. But if the painter sees something about the subject that interests him, he will make a good start. His pictures may show signs of struggle, but that isn't bad. The thing that comes easily is not interesting for long.

My response is probably intellectual and analytical, but this doesn't have to be *the* approach. I see the painting in its totality. I may make dozens of sketches for the final illustration. I am involved in a game of fitting together a pattern or jigsaw puzzle of my own devising. This does not come together mechanically but is always dominated by the dramatic idea of the story. If the picture is to include several figures, parts of them may be eloquent, other parts less so. Since in publications the final printed page is a very expensive property, your aim should be to eliminate dead areas wherever possible. In this way, you increase the picture's vitality. People say I include everything but the kitchen sink. If this is meant critically, I cannot accept it. The only criterion, I think, is whether the result is confusion or order. The reason I plan a picture thoroughly is to avoid confusion later on.

? *How, would you say, has the camera influenced art?*

a It has done three things. It has enabled the artist to observe action that he couldn't possibly study otherwise. It has helped him gather candid material for documentation—the material that will not remain still and submit to prolonged observation. And it has

Gettysburg. Mixed media. *Look*

provided a way to get a great deal out of a model in
one sitting. It would be silly not to use the camera.
You can hire a model for one hour and in that time
get a great many poses and variations of them. We can
research our figure poses just as we do interiors or
battlefields. My pictures are very complicated
compositionally. I may have one hundred figures in
one picture. The organization of these figures is what
challenges me, and I am grateful to the camera as an
aid to research. Not long ago I went down to the Civil
War country to take pictures so I could document my
drawings. I wanted to be this thorough because there
are so many experts on the Civil War around. We
must remember, however, that the photograph is not
a substitute for drawing. The camera has, in fact,
benefited the artist most because it can record the
actual scene so accurately. This releases the artist
to go into entirely different channels, leaving
absolute realism to the camera.

? *Don't you ever do a picture just for fun?*

a Sometimes. I don't know if it's any better than the
stuff I do for pay. Illustration is an art form
I respect. The illustrator is a picture-maker-for-hire
as were all great artists of the past so he is in
excellent company. We illustrators serve the writer.
Our job is to arrest the page flipper and start him
reading. The person who picks up a magazine stops at
the illustration—or should stop—and look over to
read the title and author's name. The minute he starts
84   reading the first paragraph our job is done. We may

choose to illustrate a very minor point in the story, but if it succeeds in making someone read the piece, this is justified.

It is my contention that we commercial artists are the only professional artists, in the old sense of the word, who are left. And to be successful as a professional artist one has to walk a tightrope—to achieve the greatest remuneration with the minimum compromise. Let's take the artist who paints portraits. The family of the subject thinks, "That doesn't look like Emmy's mouth." But the painter has put it down that way because that's the way he sees it, and that's how it should stay. He shouldn't compromise and change it. Whistler once said to someone who complained that the mouth wasn't right, "You can fix that when you get home." His definition of a portrait was, "a picture in which there's something the matter with the mouth."

Robert Fawcett

? *You have stressed the importance of an "obedient hand" as well as an accurate eye. How can the student develop a drawing hand that will do what he wants to do?*

a I would advise him to spend every spare moment developing the coordination of his eye and his hand to acquire greater resources for what is a difficult business at best. He should not be content with a few sketches, framed and hung. He should make hundreds, thousands, of complete studies, action sketches, composition notes and accurate observations about the visible world around him. After long practice it will no longer be necessary for him to draw these things, his eye will be always observant and his brain trained to remember. But that time is probably far away so he should draw constantly, freely, searchingly, courageously, experimentally, lovingly. But forever draw because what he puts down is the measure of what he has seen. The more he draws, the more he will see.

I tell students not to seek formulas. They have no value for the serious student. Make no excuses about materials. They are unimportant. Use those at hand to the limit of their possibilities. Cheap paper and a medium pencil are good for studies. Never stop short of completion and never be afraid of "overworking." Don't stop to admire a partly completed sketch. Try to see what it lacks. Act boldly and firmly, do not be tentative. Let each stroke be a positive statement. Work long and searchingly on a subject which seems

Story illustration. Mixed media. *Collier's*

to demand it, striving for accuracy. As the student develops he will do these things instinctively. Only the mature person becomes the mature artist.

? *Do you ever doodle out an idea?*

a Yes. After I read a manuscript which I am to illustrate I let my pencil or pen just wander around making random marks. All I am doing is ruminating quietly and letting errant ideas appear. Most of these pages wind up in the trash basket. But eventually one picture will emerge—the right one.

? *What do you look for in a picture?*

a Pictorial interest. Music excites the ear. It's hard to define. So pictures excite the eye. It seems to

**Robert
Fawcett**

me as simple as that. It has nothing to do with its
subject matter, it's content. A Beethoven quartet
isn't saying anything. It's just there. What use is
a Beethoven quartet? To feed the spirit, to feed the
soul. By the same token a picture represents what a
man does with his picture materials. It, too, should
feed the soul. There is the imagination working in the
abstract. To say that subject matter is important is
to say that a picture of a diamond necklace is more
important than one of a tin can. Of course, subject
matter does influence the forms and rhythms of a
picture. If you're doing a battle scene, you have one
thing, and the picture of a little girl sitting by a
pool will be quite another thing.

I believe that the qualities that have made some
paintings better than others have always been abstract
qualities. I don't think the absence of subject matter
makes a thing abstract.

? *What satisfaction do you get out of being an
illustrator? Is it professional pride in your own
accomplishment as an artist or are you pleased with
the public response to your pictures?*

a It is gratifying to know that one sometimes has an
audience of ten million people a week. And in every
country of the world. Many have written me letters.
I know they are looking at my work, evaluating it,
clipping, and saving it.

If you want to be an artist, you will be an artist.
If you do not become one, there's nobody you can
blame but yourself. The techniques can be learned
and *should* be learned thoroughly. Then comes the
relentless application of your knowledge.

9

ERNEST FIENE

**22 famous
painters
and
illustrators
tell how
they work**

Photograph of the artist

Ernest Fiene's colorful paintings are exhibited in thirty-two public collections, from the great New York museums to the Library of Congress, from Terre Haute, Indiana to Tel Aviv. They hang in the Metropolitan Museum, the Whitney, the Museum of Modern Art, and the Brooklyn Museum. Fiene has won countless awards and honors for his work, including the Norman W. Harris Prize of the Chicago Art Institute and the W. A. Clark Prize of the Corcoran Gallery, Washington, D.C. More than sixty publications have written about or published his work. Whether he is painting the gentle Connecticut countryside, Manhattan turbulence, or the coast of Maine, Fiene endows his pictures with personal concern. He is always, and visibly, involved with his subject, whatever it may be. As a consequence, his paintings are notable for their warmth and sense of immediacy. Born in Germany, he emigrated to the United States in 1912 and became a U.S. citizen in 1928. He studied at the National Academy of Design in New York for four years and the Beaux Arts Institute of New York for two. Later he attended the Art Students League and L'Académie de LaGrande Chaumière in Paris. Fiene has taught at Cooper Union, the Art Students League, and the Ogunquit School of Painting and Sculpture. After serving as President of Artists Equity Association, he was elected Honorary President of the New York Chapter. He lives in New York City but travels widely.

Color

I just feel happy when I express myself through pigment. It is the greatest forgetfulness in the world. I find myself more easily and completely through painting than through any other activity. The idea of putting that gray-green against that yellow, it excites me. Look at this picture of the sea. A lot of people might say, "You dope, that's just a mustard-colored ocean." It isn't! It's a painting.

? *Do you see the end result as soon as you begin a painting?*

a I definitely have the thing in mind as soon as I begin to paint. I visualize the composition and the various color relationships. But I may not be right because

The Wreck No. 3. Oil. Nelson A. Rockefeller Collection

once I put the color in that influences the next step, often many adjustments have to be made.

? *In your work, the color is used so powerfully. Do you have a strong individual theory about utilizing color in art?*

a In nature, color is light. In paint, color is merely a pigment and should be heightened. One should not copy nature in the picture. It would be too dull. Because the very pigment itself darkens in time, the pigment has to be used in a fresh way and not mixed and mixed until there is only an imitation of a surface of nature. Imitation is not the intent of the artist. After hundreds of years, colors should still be fresh and vivid. The old masters used color that way, not as imitation but as creation.

? *What was your early training? Did you always want to be an artist?*

a As far back as I can remember I drew and painted and liked it very much. I came to the United States from Germany in 1912 when I was eighteen years old.

Ernest Fiene

I went to the National Academy in New York. I also used to go to lectures by William Chase and Robert Henri. They were great influences on me. But the National Academy gave me excellent training. Leon Kroll taught the antiquity class. Sundays I attended his painting class. In those days, tuition was free in the National Academy School, but to be accepted you had to pass an examination. One had to start at the bottom, drawing from antique figures for a year, then graduating to the life drawing class. The drawings had to pass an examination before the student entered the life painting class.

? *Did you find this disciplined approach frustrating in any way?*

a Not at all. The beauty of antique figures is like nothing else. Whether it is a depiction of a young goddess or an old character, it is perfection. You know what a foot is and a hand is when you have that kind of discipline behind you. I wouldn't say I consider this the only way to train artists, but it is a most difficult thing to teach students how to paint who don't know how to draw. Drawing takes a very long discipline. Whether it should be drawing from antique figures or not, I don't know.

? *I take it that you believe drawing is the foundation of fine art?*

a I say to my students if you can't draw it, you can't paint it. A student may answer, "I don't like to draw. I want to paint." Those who are serious will take the discipline and learn to draw. Of course, students must also learn to see.

The only thing that will help a student is to learn how to see. It is more important than learning how to do. To teach a student how to see and to cultivate his eye is perhaps the most important contribution a teacher can make. The student is apt to paint what he knows, this influences his observation. Many times I say to a student, "Why do you draw what you don't see? The head turns this way. You make it turn the other way. This shoulder line turns up, not down the way you drew it." It is hard for them to shorten limbs in foreshortening, because they think of the normal size. I urge them to look at the masters, not to imitate them but to see how great art is constructed.

Yesterday, Today, and Tomorrow. Oil. Collection of Paul Fiene

?　*When you started on your career, did you expect to make a living at art?*

a　Having to earn a living I applied what knowledge
I had. I worked for a painter who painted decorative
pictures. He was a Beaux Arts painter who did mostly
murals. He was not very good at figure work so I did
that for him. I also made copies of Rembrandt,
Fragonard, and the old masters from originals at the
Metropolitan. People used to buy these copies to hang
in their drawing rooms. They liked elegance then,
modern art was not fashionable. I managed to make a
living. I was painting constantly. I got a place in
Woodstock and worked. I didn't like to have a job.

? *Was it a struggle?*

a Very much of a struggle. I considered myself a modern in those days. Until World War II, I was considered a modern on the American scene.

**Ernest
Fiene**

? *Can you pinpoint any influence that had a major effect on your style?*

a My influences were legion, among them the old masters and the Postimpressionists. At that time, so many of the painters were imitating the style of Cézanne. I got quite tired of it and decided to do something else. In 1926, I began to paint American scenes, specifically scenes of New York City. One of them, which you may have seen in the Whitney Museum, of the Dyckman Church was very gray and somber. It made quite a sensation at the time.

? *Was this somber key a reflection of your mood at that period?*

a Very definitely. I wanted to find my own reality. This mood runs through later paintings, a series I did of Connecticut churches. I was trying to achieve the clean and classical expression of the style of the church. I painted all the seasons of the year during this period. Actually, I had my choice of a great variety of subject matter. I also did still life and portraits.

? *Did you enjoy portrait painting?*

a Very much. I like to paint people, their character, their reality. I believe in portraiture, and I feel that each picture must be thoroughly realized.

? *You have done a number of self-portraits. What value is there in painting yourself?*

a There are two ways of looking at it. You don't have a model so you can always be your own model. The other is self-dissecting, inspecting yourself. Rembrandt's self-portraits are the perfect example of that.

? *During the thirties you were well known as a social realist, weren't you?*

a I was not a social-scene painter in the accepted use of the term. Yet in 1935, I was commissioned to be an art

New Snow. Oil. The Metropolitan Museum of Art.
George A. Hearn Fund, 1943

expert for the Resettlement Administration in
Washington. Ben Shahn was there also. For this job,
I went to West Virginia and made paintings of ghost
towns. In my free time, I painted quite a few pictures
for myself. I never went into the propaganda part of
the social-scene painting, just the pictorial part.
Just before that time I went to Italy on a Guggenheim
Fellowship to study Piero della Francesca. I studied
fresco painting in Florence, and later this led into
another field—mural painting. I did murals for the
government. But the one job that stands out is the
mural I painted for the High School of Needletrades.
It is the largest mural in New York City. It contains
at least fifty portraits of such figures of the time
as FDR, Herbert Lehman, Lillian Wald, David
Dubinsky, Sidney Hillman, Justice Brandeis, all the
people who contributed to reform in the garment
industry.

**Ernest
Fiene**

? *Are you ever worried about what to paint? Or do you
find you have no problem finding a subject?*

a There is no doubt that the problem of what to paint is
one of mental obstruction—the obstruction being that
the student remembers paintings with grandiose
subjects. Since his surroundings do not contain these
subjects ready-made, he despairs of finding a subject
worthy of great effort.

Artists of all periods have painted their
environments. It may have been the Roman
campagna, the flatlands of Holland, or just their plain
little home towns. Each of these has its own quality,
and, when interpreted by the mind of the artist,
paintings of them have increased our appreciation of
life, art, and humanity.

There's no place that isn't paintable. But you
should paint the subject you know best. Avoid
painting scenes you remember from other pictures.

Sometimes you don't see the possibilities in a
subject. There are many places I've been and not seen
a picture. The light wasn't right or the mood wasn't
right and then all of a sudden it is right and the
picture is there and exciting. There are so many
angles you can work from, which the inexperienced
eye does not see.

? *After deciding on a subject to paint how do you
approach it, technically or emotionally?*

a My feeling about the subject is predominant. My
emotional reaction is direct. I want to organize the
subject and create a picture that expresses what
I feel about the subject.

? *Do you make sketches and then work from them in
your studio?*

a Many of my small paintings are done directly on the
spot. For the larger compositions, I make many
drawings, generally in pencil. I write in the color
notes. Later I paint the picture in my studio.

I make all kinds of sketches on the scene. Some
sketches I just can't wait to get at, others I may not
use for years. This one of old lobster houses is an
example. I made this sketch twelve years ago and
finally made the picture only last week.

95

Queen Anne's Lace and Pomedory. Oil. Courtesy of Midtown Gallery

? *Your work has always reflected your feelings about America and your personal environment. What do you find for subject matter today?*

a I paint wherever I am. I paint what I feel and see and experience whether it is drab or elegant. I try to paint what I care about deeply. I may go off to a place like the Pennsylvania Dutch Country or Maine or Cape Cod because I have an affinity for these places. After all, you make your environment where you are happy. The fact that these places yield many ideas for pictures is probably important, too. However, I don't agree with some people who think that only a few special subjects are pictorial subjects. I feel that any subject makes a picture. To make a beautiful picture you don't have to paint the most beautiful women in the world. I've done a lot of industrial subjects that, to the average person, would not seem suitable for pictures. I love to do them.

? *Can you define realistic art?*

Ernest Fiene

a It is a recognizable subject matter organized in a pictorial way. Abstract art is abstracted from life. Whether it is condensed or simplified or whether you are presenting the core of the subject, you've still taken it from life. I believe that painting is a visual art, and it should have an association with nature.

I consider nonobjective art to be a decorative art. It is very interesting, but there is no humanity in it. One might even call it the expression of man's conceit. I also believe the picture has to speak for itself; people should be able to read it without explanation.

? *Do you collect art?*

a Yes, I have Lachaise drawings and some by Roualt and Pascin, lithographs that attracted me of all the artists of the thirties. I have pre-Columbian sculpture, African sculpture, and other sculpture. I am looking for subjective response, all kinds of style, and subject matter. I like to surround myself with pictures and sculpture.

? *Do you ever feel like giving up on painting?*

a When I have doubts about life, then I also have doubts about art. But I'm never happier than when I'm painting.

I try to communicate through my painting the life we are living in this period of history. I like to record my environment and my reaction to the environment through the medium of paint in a technically permanent way. Traditionally this has been the function of art. This is why I am not interested in imitating old masters. I wish to paint my own life, and I consider myself a continuity not a reaction. You grow through observation. You begin to understand life by study and observation. It's a tough process. I have a kind of universal attitude toward art. I am interested in the whole broad field of art. I suppose you could sum up my philosophy this way. I believe with William Blake that the only sin is limitation.

97

10

GEORGE GIUSTI

**22 famous
painters
and
illustrators
tell how
they work**

Photograph of the artist

In the years since 1938 when he came to America from Europe, George Giusti has established himself as one of this country's leading designers. He has received more than thirty important awards in the field of design. He has taken gold medals, silver medals, awards, and citations from his fellows in the graphic arts field. Among his prizes are ones from the Art Directors Club of Philadelphia, the Chicago Art Directors Club, the Art Directors Club of Milwaukee, the Art Directors Club of New York, the American Institute of Graphic Arts, and the Pittsburgh Art Directors Club. In 1958 Giusti was elected "Art Director of the Year" and given the "Golden T-Square Award" of the National Society of Art Directors. He has had portfolios published in Europe, Japan, and the United States. His exhibitions have traveled to the important capitals of the world through the good offices of the Art Directors Club and the U.S. State Department. Giusti and his wife divide their time between a summer home in Mendham, New Jersey and a New York City studio-apartment.

Design

Even if design today is understood more or less as designing furniture or cars or fashion, I think it is fair to call the sort of thing I do "design." I don't design products, but I do actually design editorial and advertising material. Design is, after all, a matter of constructive thinking.

? *And editing down?*

a Yes indeed. Design is the materialization of an idea. It is a statement; it is a conception. A package may not want to "say anything" besides being pleasant and conveying the feeling of the product.

The client or the agency will tell you: "We need a series of twelve ads for this particular product or a package for this preparation that is going to be sent to doctors." It is your problem to figure out what can be done. For this you should know people, have a certain feeling for human relations.

? *Are you afraid of being typecast or being so good with your particular style that you won't have a chance to do anything else?*

a Most of the time when somebody comes to me with an assignment he doesn't say, "I saw your *Fortune* cover. That's just what we want." They come to me because

Graphis No. 78. India ink and dyes

they know what my potentialities are. What I do for
Fortune is different from what I do for *Holiday*,
except for the quality and the seriousness of the work.
I don't think that these are mere technical
achievements.

If I feel I have done the job in a right way, in a
dignified way, I have satisfaction. If I take a job,
it is because it interests me. The product is of value
to somebody, and it is my task to interpret it in my
own way. I do not believe in the theory of "L'art
pour l'art." A painter has always had a boss, a job
to do that has been commissioned by somebody else.
It is up to him to do it the way he feels it and not
follow the dictation of the client.

George Giusti

? *How were you trained? As a designer or as a painter?*

a Actually I was trained to be an architect. I went to the Academy of Breva in Milan where I learned all the rudiments of art as well—perspective, drawing, painting. It was very strict formal training. We did everything, copying of casts, studying anatomy. We visited hospitals to learn anatomy. It was very thorough training, training from the ground up.

? *Did you become interested in design while you were at the Academy or later?*

a While I was studying, I got interested in graphics and advertising. I started to visit a studio after school hours. Any time I would have a couple of hours free, I would go to the studio and help them with any kind of problem they would have. I worked on newspaper advertisements, booklets, posters.

? *Was this the way you acquired your practical knowledge of design, by serving an apprenticeship?*

a Yes, I did get it that way. I wanted to put the theoretical learning of the Academy to work. At that time in Italy a student at the Academy didn't have a chance to work practically on projects. Besides the artistic curriculum, we had to study mathematics, chemistry, literature, and history. It was a strict education, really very complex. Even today although they have modern painters and sculptors teaching instead of more conservative academicians it is still strict training. At the time I went, they wouldn't let us go into the progressive aspects of art. On my own I began to be acquainted with the Futurists. I visited the galleries and studios of painters. The Cubists and the Futurists were not as accepted then as now. They had to fight very hard for recognition.

? *Why did you decide to study art? Were there artists in your family?*

a I wanted to become a surgeon, or a doctor, but I couldn't afford the long studies. Art interested me just as much so I decided to become an artist.

? *Did you draw as a boy?*

a I suppose I always drew as a boy. I started very early. Before the Academy, I went to a technical school. It was directed toward engineering, something not at all

Rome. Dyes.
Reprinted by special permission of *Holiday*.
© 1960 The Curtis Publishing Company

attractive to me at that time. So I took another direction, into art.

? *What would you say is the ideal curriculum for someone who wants to study design?*

a Well, he should study the fundamental theory of design—division of space, balance, relationship between elements, color, technique, drawing. I think academic drawing is very important as a discipline.

? *How did you move into the design field after you acquired formal training?*

George Giusti

a Slowly. I just concentrated on the studio job and after some time, a year, two years, I went to Switzerland and worked in a studio as a designer. It was an arrangement that combined the American concept of an advertising agency and the art studio. In an American advertising agency, they have a couple of layout men, but they don't concentrate on really designing material. The agency will usually call in a free-lance artist. In the studio, on the other hand, there is a kind of "house style." Everything that comes out of the studio has certain characteristics. To put it in another way, the advertising agency people are more or less businessmen with an understanding of design. The art director in an advertising agency doesn't have time to sit down and do the job. Of course if it comes to routine paste-ups then they have a few young artists who work in the agency. A studio, on the other hand, is built around a group of artists. They unite. They have a common agent, and the agent goes out and gets them work. In my Swiss studio, we had several designers. It was my first real contact with the art business and my first contact with typography.

? *Why did you choose Switzerland as the country in which to make a professional start?*

a Although I was born in Milan, my nationality was Swiss. In Switzerland, they have a very long history of doing good design. They are in a fortunate geographic position in the center of Europe. If anything happens in France or England in the field of graphics, they know about it immediately. They are well informed.

? *What would you say about America's position in the design field?*

a This country has something Europe doesn't have— youth. It is wide open here with more room for new ideas. It is wonderful to have a deep tradition like the Europeans, but they are sometimes slowed down by it. They don't dare do something completely illogical. This country has more room for experimentation. Switzerland, for example, is well known for its taste in printing, posters, and advertising, but they are at a stage now where it is all too perfect. There is no room for mistakes, and when there is no room for mistakes, there is no room for new ideas. The standards there are high, but they have crystallized to the point where there is no room for mistakes and no

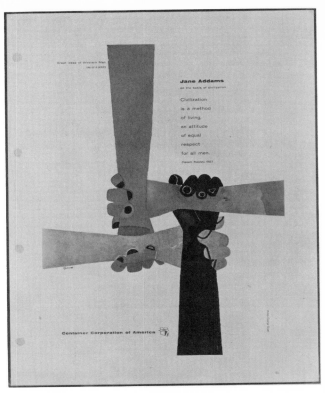

Four Hands. Dyes, tempera, and inks.
Commissioned by Container Corporation of America for
the Great Ideas of Western Man Series

room for genius. Here you may see horrible things, but
you also see strokes of genius. That is the basic
difference between a typical European country and
the United States.

Somehow it is more exciting here for a designer. He
can dare to do things. He can give everything.
However the exceptional thing may represent only a
small part of the output here. In Europe, the high
level in art is very diffuse.

? *Are the artist's relationships with his clients different
in Europe from what they are here?*

a Here it is probably more casual. In Europe, I think it
is very difficult to meet the client himself. Here you

can talk to the client. In Europe, he is kept very much in the background. He doesn't want to come out and shake hands with you. More often the client is able to accept new ideas when he is confronted directly. If you have to go through a chain of agencies and agents, he may resist an idea. If you approach him directly, he will be ready but his subordinates are not always ready.

George Giusti

? *How did your professional career progress after you went to Switzerland?*

a After I worked in the studio for a while, I opened my own studio in Zurich. I had my own clients and so forth. In 1937-38, I thought I would like to come over here. I wasn't sure I would like it enough to stay, but on the other hand if you come as a visitor, you don't put all your effort into it. If you break entirely with the old country, it is different. So that's what I did. I just liquidated my studio. I came to New York, and I worked for a friend of mine who was designing the Swiss Pavilion for the World's Fair. Then I went to Washington to design an exhibition for the government. After I finished that job, I started to look around. My first break was with *Fortune* magazine. They asked me to do a cover. It was a modern conception, as I remember. Since then I have done quite a lot of covers for *Fortune*. I started to be introduced to the advertising agencies. It was the beginning of the war in Europe, and there was rearmament here. During the war, I did quite a lot of propaganda work for the government, O.S.S., and the air force. But in between these jobs, I had a lot to do for industry. And I did a lot of institutional advertising work. That's wonderful.

? *Do you think the chances for good design in editorial illustration and advertising have improved since then?*

a When I came in 1938, it wasn't possible to buy anything modern or well designed. Now you can buy good modern products. But at that time, there simply wasn't anything in New York that could be called modern. The most modern thing was Rockefeller Center. In the last twenty years, this country has made tremendous progress. Packaging and book jackets are good examples of the influence of modern design.

THIS TOO IS MERRITT-CHAPMAN & SCOTT...**EQUIPMENT**

Advertisement. India ink and dyes. Merritt-Chapman and Scott

? *What has stimulated the interest in design?*

a The influence of the people who came here during the war. The famous architects who came and talked to students in the universities. Young people got acquainted with the principles of design. There is no reason today for old-fashioned and bad poster art. We are so up to date in packaging, beautiful publications, books, and so on. The newspapers have good advertising, far superior to European. The whole category of illustration is better than in Europe. The artists who illustrate fiction and design fashion here are really tops.

? *Would you say there was a greater market for a designer now than twenty years ago? Where are the big markets for design?*

a Even in Europe, there is a greater opportunity for designers than when I left. The Common Market has brought this about. In the old days, if you were Italian, you couldn't work in France or Germany or England, and designers in those countries couldn't work in Italy. It has all changed now. I suppose New York offers the biggest opportunity for designers. But then Los Angeles and Chicago are also big markets.

? *What advice would you give a young person embarking on a career in design?*

George Giusti

a I would advise him to get the most thorough training available. Discipline is the most important ingredient. I think it is good for a student who wants to enter the design field to try several branches instead of immediately settling down into one. He might try an advertising agency for a year, then go to work for a publishing house and see how this kind of design is done. He could work as an interior designer, or try package design. He should sample several branches of design work. I tried a little bit of everything before I found that what I do is what I like best. I think to be versatile is the best way, to be able to do packages, illustrations, book jackets.

? *When you do a cover for a magazine are you given explicit instructions as to content and general approach?*

a The editors never tell me what to do, except they do tell me what is in the issue. If, for example, the issue is devoted to the Coast Guard, then it is my job to design the cover around their subject.

? *Do you submit a rough sketch or simply the completed job?*

a I don't like to show the client a sketch and then have to copy my own sketch. I'd rather do the final picture, the first time.

? *Design is an intellectualized form of art. Do you consciously work on a problem as an intellectual exercise or do you have emotional feelings about the project?*

a To solve a problem in a graphic form the first thing is to understand the problem thoroughly. If it is a book, you must know the content of the book. If in some instances mechanical things are involved, it is better to go to the factory, get the feeling of the character of the industry. Then, I think it is a question of finding an idea. Sometimes it is just a twist of a word.

**George
Giusti**

? *Could you give me an example of how you develop an idea for, say, a* Holiday *cover?*

a Suppose it is an issue about France. What symbol conveys the feeling of France? The Eiffel Tower? The blue, the red and white? Some particular shape? You're not going to reproduce the Eiffel Tower. No, perhaps you draw a shape that would explain the subject. This is a kind of sign language. You carry a message by visual means.

? *In this simplifying how do you achieve richness?*

a By eliminating detail, I achieve impact. By using fewer colors, I attain more contrast. By simplifying shapes, I make them bolder.

? *Are you conscious of working in a way that is peculiarly your own?*

a There are probably people working in the same direction. Maybe we've all seen the same things at the same time, and we are reacting to them. Suddenly the magazines are full of red balloons or whatever, but it doesn't matter. Each artist will report it in a fresh way, each one does it differently.

I think you can't be original on purpose. If it isn't in you it just isn't there. Everybody has a period of unproductiveness. You should just be natural, be yourself. Don't try to be fancy or extravagant to cover up some deficiency. Just be honest. If at a certain time of your life you are naïve, just be naïve in your drawings. Hard work will not supply talent if it isn't there, but it will improve it if it is there.

? *Did you feel you were talented?*

a I always drew and painted, so I suppose there was a certain amount of talent. But I had to improve it with hard work.

? *What can you foresee for design in the future?*

a Industrial design has a very great future. Everything is design. Little by little it will get more sensible and better. At least industry saw the necessity of doing these things. In some cases design has deteriorated into a fashion affair. You are called a stylist instead of a designer. A stylist slaps a few fins or chrome on a car without any engineering concept. It is done to hide design deficiencies.

? *What kind of art appeals to you personally?*

a I like everything that is good or looks good to me. I have a feeling for traditional things, but since we are living now in the twentieth century, I don't think it is right to live in the manner of Versailles. You can't live as people did two or three hundred years ago. You have to force yourself to break away.

Actually, I look at a painting not only for the sake of the painting, but as something that is almost a part of the room, a structural part. I very seldom have paintings on my walls. I would have a mural. That would make sense because it would be part of the room itself. When I see pictures in a museum I try to figure out how they would look in an architectural setting. I consider them in relation to space. So far as the painting itself is concerned, there are so many things I like. I like modern painting, abstract painting, surrealist paintings, Giotto. I like the very early Greek sculptures. As long as I feel it has a deep quality, I like it. The skill of the painter, the meaning of the picture, the emotion it would convey, the message it has to offer, these are important.

? *Is commercial work—ads, illustrations—art?*

a It can be routine or it can be art. It is art if it is well done no matter what it is. A racing car can be art.

? *Are you trying to convey anything beyond a "sell" when you do a design for editorial or advertising?*

a If I do an ad for a product, my duty is to convey the feeling of the product, to communicate with the public, to tell the public why it is good for them to have this or that. I would like to do this in a series of aesthetic ways, not in a cheap way. I want always to attain a certain dignity in this communication. I want to present the product and the idea in a dignified way. Your own essential nature must come through. I know it will come through as long as I keep my principles. I don't want to make a show of myself personally, and then later think about the product and the cover. The message is what's important to me.

11

PETER HELCK

**22 famous
painters
and
illustrators
tell how
they work**

Photograph of the artist

Peter Helck is one of the great illustrators of industrial America. Racing cars, steel mills, and railroads are his favorite subjects and he is able to give them artistic dimension. The artist, however, lives far from the smoky atmosphere of the machine age. At his 200-year-old farmhouse in Boston Corners, New York, he keeps a barn full of antique automobiles and looks out on a peaceful, pastoral landscape. Peter Helck was born in New York City. He says that his first passion as a boy was the steam locomotive. Then he discovered the beauty of the automobile and from that moment on his hobby became the study and acquisition of racing cars. He witnessed the Vanderbilt Cup Race in 1906 and describes it as his biggest thrill. He is the proud owner of "Old '88," the Locomobile Racer which won the 1908 Vanderbilt Cup. By the age of twelve, Helck was attending summer classes at the Art Students League. At eighteen he had a job in the art department of a New York department store. After working in commercial studios, Helck started free-lancing in his own New York studio. Soon he had made a specialty of industrial painting. After World War I service in the Navy, he studied art in Europe and was greatly influenced by Frank Brangwyn, the famous muralist. During the next ten years, Helck's work as an artist in America was interrupted by several trips to Europe to study under Brangwyn. In 1930 his industrial paintings won the Harvard Award and he also acquired his first antique automobile—a 1904 Mercedes. In 1961 Helck completed a book on antique automobiles called *The Checkered Flag* for which he had done 120 paintings. That year he was given a one-man show at the Salmagundi Club and named "Artist of the Year."

Industrial Art

If a subject isn't intrinsically monumental I try to find some way of handling it so that it becomes monumental. For example, in the making of steel some operations aren't particularly vital pictorially. Then I resort to exaggerated perspective, improvise more dramatic lighting, innovate with color to achieve the heroic and monumental.

I distort perspective very freely. Sometimes I rearrange the elements of the picture to get more drama. Once I had to paint a train going up the valley. I shifted the tracks to the other side of the river so I could get a more exciting composition. Of course I asked the client's permission before moving his tracks.

Briarcliff Road Race. Casein-tempera. Collection of the artist

? *Have you always painted in a strong affirmative style,*
or did you experiment with other styles along the way?

a As a youngster I was tremendously impressed with
German poster art. It had powerful light-and-shade
contrasts, amazing simplification, forceful design.
I liked all work that had the sense of strength and
vigor. I became a worker in this Teutonic "flat tint"
method of expression because of the dynamic effects
that resulted. It is true that those men were more
interested in design than in any human-interest angle.
But design is very important, and we can learn a great
deal from them. Before World War I, the work of a
half a dozen good American designers derived from
this art, but our entry into the war moderated this
influence. Today, however, there is a similar drive
toward vivid, startling effects via such simplified means.
We have achieved a "poster style."

112   **?** *Why do you draw in such a representational manner?*

a Why? Because my training and interests have been concerned with things as they are. Also, since so much of my work has to do with industrial subject matter, these customers, engineers mostly, expect logical portrayals. I try to stay fairly close to what I see around me,

I think I like anything that is big structurally—a building, a tractor, a locomotive, anything that has the aspect of the monumental. When I travel abroad I look for a man-made structural aspect of the scene—an old Roman bridge, a windmill. If it's set in a beautiful landscape, so much the better.

I try to make a picture that will generate a feeling of impact, something that will stop a person and keep him from turning the page.

The first thing I think of is how to make an agreeable composition. I arrange the elements in such a way that they relate directly and agreeably. I try always to use the minor elements to supplement the major ones. This takes patience and care. In composing pictorial elements you are emotionally absorbed in the creative process. Of course, craft is involved, too, because you must be able to handle your tools. Craft has little to do with first creative steps. Craft can, however, be of great help in achieving an emotional content after the preliminary organizing stages have been solved.

I can visualize the thing in lines and tones, but I can't always see the color. I may rework the colors, subordinating one and bringing up another. It is something that more or less develops as I go along.

Like everyone else engaged in the task of making pictures, I learn all I can about the subject before I begin to paint. If it happens to be a subject I am familiar with, like automobiles, I have tremendous files right at home to work from. Otherwise, I have to go out and learn all I can about it.

? *You said that firsthand research is well worth it despite the time it takes. Could you explain why?*

a I think the artist needs to saturate himself in his subject. He should go to the scene whenever possible and see for himself what its possibilities are. If he is actually there, seeing the place, noting its colors, its compositional opportunities, the flavor of the scene, he can't help but make a better picture. Of course, when you are doing a period piece you can't go back to the scene because it has disappeared. But you can do careful research and dig up whatever historical

Peter Helck

Speed in the Rain. Casein-tempera. Collection of the artist

documents will aid you in portraying the period
accurately. I did an old-time motoring subject some
years ago that also involved a steam roller of the
1907 era. I traced this steam roller to a firm in
Springfield, Ohio, and they sent me steel engravings
of rollers made by them at that time. Thanks to them
I was able to be exact in my drawing of the roller.
The president of the firm became interested in my
search and wrote me a very amusing letter. It seems
my request opened up a new hobby for him. He
enjoyed the old cars in my painting so much that he
became interested in them and started his own
collection of antique automobiles.

? *Do you think illustrators are more research-minded
today than they used to be?*

a I imagine that we are. The photograph has had a
powerful effect on art. If it's a photo it's considered
factual. This has forced the illustrator to be factual,
too. There have been artists who have been a little
less than scrupulous about their research. I think
it's dangerous. There are too many experts in all
fields and they love to take pen in hand and write.
I had to make a picture for the *Post* some years ago
having to do with a cargo ship. I got permission to
go aboard one in New York harbor and I took an
ex-merchant officer friend along for guidance. After

the illustration was published, the *Post* sent me a
letter from an old seaman who claimed that my cargo
rigging was all wrong. This and all other details had
been okayed by my officer friend. Anyway, I thanked
the complaining seaman by letter and asked him
seriously if I could retain his services—professionally—
in future ship assignments. He answered right away
and said he thought I must be a "pretty good guy" to
take his blasting criticism in that spirit. Trying to do
an honest job of research has its complications.

? *Someone once said that your pictures are as precisely
accurate in every detail as a human being can make
them. Doesn't this take a great deal of time?*

a Yes. But it's worth it. The last time I did a steel
advertisement, I made half a dozen trips down to the
mills. For hours I hung around the particular
operation I was supposed to paint. I was accompanied
by an executive who could explain the operation to me.
I'm sorry to say I really know very little about the
technology of the thing, only what I need to know in
order to make my picture valid pictorially. People
think I'm an expert on automobiles and could make
repairs. I'm sensitive to the external aesthetics of
the automobile, but am not even sure what makes the
wheels go around.
This hobby of mine has grown so fantastically
I can't see the end of it. I had a few antique cars long
before it became a popular hobby. Now everybody's
collecting them, going to rallies and racing the old
cars. I'm tickled to death to be a part of it.
All of us have some kind of hobby. If one is found
that gives the opportunity to exercise your love of
drawing and painting, so much the better. But
specializing too narrowly can be dangerous. You might
get to be known only as the fellow who draws birds or
flowers, or landscapes, and no other assignments will
come your way.
I think that a work of art can be made of anything
at all. It's the way you approach it. Anything that
excites you, that creates a terrific drive to set the
subject down on paper, is worth painting. We have all
had the experience of seeing something that arrests us
completely. For me it's automobiles and machinery.
The painter should analyze for himself precisely what
it is that causes him to feast his eyes. This will
probably make a picture.
As he works on the picture it will develop its own
character. I'll never stop being amazed by what seems

Advertisement. Casein-tempera. National Steel Corporation

sheer magic—the way that solving one problem color
area invariably indicates the solution to a neighboring
area. Like most artists, I work rapidly at the outset
to cover the entire picture area, to be rid of the
disturbing whites of the raw illustration board or
canvas. Only then do I feel the picture is under way.

? *The important thing, you said, was the approach, not
the subject matter. Could you explain?*

a You must approach a subject with enough interest and
enthusiasm to envision, or better still, actually see,
the given subject in a variety of moods. Some
assignments fail to provide such interest immediately.
I recall one at a huge Midwest distillery. Here was a
bleak array of pink brick buildings with diminutive
figures rolling barrels on tilted runways from
warehouse to truck. I saw it in bleaching sunlight and
felt no attraction for the job. Twenty-four hours
later with the coming of rain, the same scene was
unbelievably handsome: stormy sky, rose-colored brick,

sparkling reflections, gleaming rubber garments of the barrel-rollers! One's approach should be open-minded. What seems dull stuff may turn out to be inspirational.

Since the client is paying the bill I think he should be given a lot of consideration. But some artists will surrender at the first sign that a client isn't pleased. Recently, I did four racing pictures. In one I put a pole in a position that contributed to the composition. The client said he didn't like the pole there. I said I would think about it but that I believed it belonged there. (The painting was delivered *with* the pole, because I thought it made a better picture. Apparently the client agreed because there were no arguments.) You must stand firm if you believe you are justified.

Peter Helck

? *How did you happen to make art your career? Specifically, why did you choose illustration?*

a When I was a kid, we were quite poor. I drew constantly. I had what was termed "talent." There wasn't money for long art schooling. Because a job was necessary, I sought and found employment in an art department. I was aware of the financial rewards possible in commercial art, and the dimmer prospects for a youngster to make a living in the fine arts. So I became an illustrator. I've been fortunate, thanks to this profession, in being able to do things that appeal to me.

? *Was your art training adequate or would you rather have had another kind?*

a Now I probably would train differently because of changing times, altering tastes. What I learned was most useful at the time. I had highly orthodox school training, plaster casts and all that. I had practical training in six or seven art departments where I did everything from borders and lettering to twenty-four sheet posters. As a mural assistant I worked on surfaces fifteen feet wide and fifty feet long. The most gratifying schooling came in night classes of figure drawing after I began my career.

I believe the art student should know all the fundamentals of drawing, color, and perspective. He should possess or acquire a sense of design or composition. He should go to exhibitions and galleries and see the best. We have to assume that if he is a student at all he has examined the great paintings. I don't see how he could miss doing this. But I think that a student is apt to be attracted by

Advertisement. Casein-tempera. National Steel Corporation

the superficial—by the way the tools were handled.
The thing the young student should think of is not
only the way a picture was done, but why it was done.
Of course the tools are important, but you need much
more than this. Instead of being obsessed with the
technical aspects of another man's work, you must
keep in mind the need of evolving your own personal
way of doing things.

? *Do you think experimental art has a beneficial
influence on illustration?*

a As a result of some of the wild stuff connected with
modern art, commercial artists are more daring in
their use of color. Of course, there's a great deal of
fraud and incompetence in modern art. And yet, even
in these abstractions the color is frequently terrific
and the composition very satisfying.
  The by-product of much present-day experimental
painting has been beneficial. I'm glad a lot of it has
happened. But I'm highly critical about the people
who write about today's painting. They read all sorts
of things into such work, things of which the artist,
while creating it, was entirely innocent.

? *Is originality essential to success as an illustrator?*

a I suppose if a fellow studied very carefully he might
stumble on the fact that there is really very little
that is new. The new look in illustration is more the
result of magazine design and typography. There are
plenty of fellows who will make a good living doing

nothing original. Others will attempt things that they haven't done before because they feel the need to innovate. A series of very effective advertising drawings now appearing have been viewed as the New Look. However, they had been anticipated sixty years ago in Europe. The resemblance is very marked. While there is very little that is really new, it is desirable always to experiment.

Peter Helck

You have to try new things or you'll get stale. At least *I* have to. In my book *The Checkered Flag* there are about 120 Peter Helck illustrations. I tried various ways of doing them. Of course, in many there is a tendency to work in a familiar medium.

? *How important is discipline to an artist?*

a It helps. Some kids do very little with this thing called talent, and others develop facility by hard work. Practice is what makes the difference.

I think that unless a student is willing to give everything to the study of art, if there is anything that jeopardizes or challenges his dedication, he ought to stay out of it. There are too many others who do have this zeal. He may be talented and all that, but if he isn't working unremittingly, he'll never get anywhere. In other words, it's simply got to be all-absorbing.

? *Are you satisfied with your productivity as an illustrator?*

a I'll be candid. There are very few occasions when I feel any great satisfaction. I always feel my pictures have not matched the visualization I had in mind. Only rarely do I do something that genuinely pleases me. It is gratifying to get a telegram from a client telling you he likes the picture. But the greatest joy comes from those rare moments when the picture clicks. I wish it happened more often.

? *What principal advice would you give to a young artist?*

a I'll repeat what I said before. Unless it's a major obsession in his life, unless he's just pouring the stuff out all the time, he should be wary. Art is a very competitive field. Even in his late seventies Brangwyn always carried a sketchbook in his pocket. Dong Kingman has hundreds of sketchbooks loaded with pictures. The student who is that much interested in drawing is bound to accomplish something worthwhile.

119

12

DONG KINGMAN

**22 famous
painters
and
illustrators
tell how
they work**

Photograph of the artist

Dong Kingman's water colors have been described as "forceful and dynamic, sparkling with light and humor; executed with the brilliancy of an Oriental miniaturist, they transport the viewer into a world of fantasy." Kingman has won virtually every award offered for the water color medium. His works are exhibited in more than twenty-five museums, including the Museum of the Modern Art, the Metropolitan Museum and the Whitney. He has won, among other awards, the Audubon Gold Medal of Honor, the Pennell Medal at the Pennsylvania Academy of Fine Arts, an award at the American Water Color Society Exhibition and one at a special Water Color Exhibition at the Metropolitan Museum. Kingman is a member of the National Academy. Dong Kingman was born in San Francisco, the son of an impoverished Chinese family. When he was five his father moved the family to Hong Kong where he opened a store. At the age of eighteen Dong moved back to San Francisco, where he supported himself by working as a house-boy. In his free time he painted. Dong got his first break as a painter when the W.P.A. gave him an assignment in 1935. That same year he had his first one-man show in the corner of an obscure San Francisco library. In 1942 he moved to New York City and won his first Guggenheim Award. The following year he won another Guggenheim. In 1946 he was appointed to the faculty at Columbia University, where he is still teaching art. In 1948 he joined the faculty at Hunter College and taught there for five years. New York City is his permanent residence, but he travels widely both here and abroad.

Water Color

I learned to paint like my ancestors. The Chinese use only one medium—water color. To me, it is the most convenient medium if you want to do outdoor sketching. It is compact to carry and the wash dries almost immediately.

I suppose the reason I have always worked in water color is, simply, that it is right for my temperament. Every individual has a particular way of doing things, and he must find the medium that gives him the freedom to express himself well. When I paint in oil, the painting tends to get sticky. When I work in water color, I can keep it fresh. You know how it is in music. One person chooses to play the piano and another violin. Whatever suits you best is what you should adopt.

Left Bank. Water color. Collection of Albert Dorne

? *How do you achieve so much forcefulness and such a three-dimensional effect in your water-color paintings?*

a   I was always interested in architecture. I studied in an architect's office in Hong Kong as a boy. I am always thinking of things in terms of plastic forms and three dimensions. I suppose this quality is what you are responding to in my pictures.

? *Your work has more than the decorative value we associate with a traditional Chinese style of work. Of course it has grace and lightness, but it also has so much vigor. How do you account for this?*

a   That is, I think, because I am an American as well as a Chinese. I was born in 1911, in Oakland, California. My family took me to Hong Kong five years later, but somehow, even while I was living in China, I always knew I was an Américan. I did return to America for good in 1929, and I am sure my painting has been influenced as much by this country as it was by the Chinese approach to art. I learned to write with a brush like any Chinese child. The most important thing a Chinese learns in school is to write with a brush or paint with a brush.

**Dong
Kingman**

? *Through your facility with a brush you have established
a distinct technique. Are you conscious of using this
technique or do you work subjectively?*

a If you don't have technique, you won't be able to
express an emotion, no matter how strongly you feel it.
I think you start out being very aware of technique.
But this becomes unconscious before long, and your
feelings about the painting become dominant. This is
probably the strongest reason why you should learn the
craft of painting. It is so frustrating to feel a picture
and not be able to execute it. My response to a
subject is unconscious and automatic, a blend of what
I have seen and what I know to be worth painting.

? *What training do you think helped you most?*

a Hard work brought results in my case. There are no
shortcuts. You have to learn about the important
principles of art. You have to practice every day.
I have been painting for forty years and I'm still
learning. Nobody ever finishes learning art. Even
when I was working in factories and as a houseboy to
support my family, I made the time to paint.

? *Did you ever have any formal art training in the
Chinese school of painting?*

a The only art teacher I ever had was a Chinese artist
named Sze-to Wai who was my teacher in 1926 at the
Lingnan School. He had gone to Paris as a young man
and returned to be headmaster at the school. He gave
me a Western approach to art as well as the traditional
Chinese training. I was painting Chinese style until
I met him. He showed me reproductions of the
Western masters—Cézanne, Matisse, Van Gogh.
   The thing he taught me I have been most grateful
for was his emphasis on simplification. "Simplify,
simplify," he used to tell me. The thing you see from
the distance must be painted in terms of the
impression it makes on the viewer, not in terms of its
complicated details, which can only be seen close up.

? *Most of your work is clearly influenced by the big city.
Do you dislike the country, or have you just lived in
cities all your life and naturally wanted to paint them?*

a I guess I am just used to the city. The architectural
forms fascinate me. Washington is the perfect place

123

Blue Moon. Water color. Courtesy of Museum of Fine Arts, Boston

for me to paint. I am intrigued by monuments and
statuary and big buildings. I have been happy painting
in Paris, Rome, Hong Kong, and, of course, New York.
There is so much going on—so many shapes and forms
and rhythms.

Painters like the French Impressionists with their
sunny, bucolic atmosphere are not good for me. But
I try to show in my paintings people sitting around
having a good time in the city. Even on a dark, dirty
waterfront there will be one spot of beauty. I want
to paint the contrast to show the two sides of life.

? *Your paintings convey a light, airy feeling. Is the
sun always out when you paint, or do you achieve this
effect in another way?*

a In my painting I always look for sunlight even if there
is none around me. A feeling of sunlight is a happy
feeling. It may not be the academic way of doing
things to manufacture sunlight in a place where
sunlight could not possibly fall. Logically, it's not
right, but if it creates the mood and effect I want, it
makes sense to me. It is important to know how to
lighten a picture, because if you have no contrast
between dark and light, you have nothing.

? *By "inventing" the sunlight, so to speak, you are simply exercising poetic license?*

a This is a thing you learn to do from experience.

? *A fellow artist once said of you, "He is really amazing! He can see pattern in anything, whether it is a tuft of grass or a crowd of people." Were you always able to do this, or did it develop after you became practiced in seeing?*

a You have to see the pattern in the things around you. This is not necessarily a special experience for me. It can be shared by most people who take the trouble to train their eye to see form and shape. We all live surrounded by beauty. We don't see it because we are not trained to look for it. Actually, every subject under the sun is worth painting. You shouldn't be put off by an object because it is familiar. Look what the great painters have done with the apple, for example. The important thing is what you do with the subject, how you express yourself.

? *Composition is a crucial element in a good painting. What does the term mean to you?*

a To me it means the overall pattern, the relationship of the large areas to the small, the rhythms of the painting. Actually the hardest part of composition is making the large element go with the small. You have to work these things out to sustain interest in the painting.

? *For example?*

a I never try to put a whole element in a painting in the most obvious way. If I have a cow, I hang a towel in front of her so you don't see all of her.

? *When you put so much into each painting, so many elements, isn't it hard to compose the painting?*

a That is true. But actually the simplest picture is the hardest to paint. Chinese painting is pure stroke.

? *How do you go about composing a picture, or can't you really analyze it?*

a First, you deliberately break up the picture, and then you get it all together again.

New York Harbor. Water color. Private collection

? *How do you get it all together again?*

a That is the hardest part. First I put down my elements. Then I see what large areas I need to bring them all together. A dark tone over one area can draw them together.

? *Can you tell at the outset how a picture will come together?*

a You always visualize the end result and hope it will come off. You have that dream that it will. But as you work, new images come to you, and the picture may go in another direction.

? *How often do you go out with your sketch pad?*

a I go out sketching every day when the weather is good. I go to Central Park or Washington Square or the East River when I am in New York. When I am traveling, I make hundreds of sketches of what interests me, and then I take them home and make finished compositions of the best of them.

? *When you take notes by sketching out on location, how do you know if you have enough to go on later, when you are making the picture at home?*

a I can't stop sketching until I get enough identification of the place. Otherwise, I would not be able to carry it through at home.

Dong Kingman

? *Do you finish one painting at a time?*

a I have thirty or forty going at once. Maybe I won't touch one for three months while I think about it. Maybe it will be finished the next day. Everything is going at once.

? *You often paint the same scene over again. Why do you return to the same subject matter? Are you trying to get more out of the scene or are you disciplining yourself to see it in a fresh way?*

a Some subjects I paint over and over. I painted Central Park five or six years ago, but after my return from a trip around the world, the park reminded me of something else, something I saw in London, so now I have a new approach to it. I'm not disciplining myself to see the scene in a new way. I just view it differently after I have been exposed to other experiences.

? *In other words, you take the elements you like from a given scene, but you don't feel obliged to put everything you see into a painting or put it on paper the way nature has arranged it?*

a That's about it. I take the most important thing, important to me, out of the scene. I carry many backgrounds in my head and I use them when they seem right for the picture. Things I've seen in the Orient or Paris look fine combined with a New York impression of trees or buildings.

? *Do you ever feel that your audience may be a little confused by seeing a familiar landmark in one of your pictures, but then wonder why the Eiffel Tower, say, is behind Grand Central Terminal?*

a I want them to see the picture my way. I like to take a subject and play with it. Someone compared me to a comedian who will take a familiar subject like George Washington crossing the Delaware and spin a completely different story out of it. You can take

127

Golden Gate Bridge. Water color. Private collection

something everyone recognizes and then you improvise
or embellish and create something new. I hope people
find humor in my work because I have so much fun
painting this way. I have my own way of seeing things
and this is what I want to get across.

? *Speaking of seeing things your own way, what do the
symbols in your pictures mean—those strange
neuter-type people, the use of bicycles and locomotives
and dumbbells? Are you simply having fun with these
objects or do they have some special significance to you?*

a Each one, I suppose, means something different to me.

? *What about the locomotives? What do they mean?*

a I keep asking myself why locomotives intrigue me so
much. When you are young, a train is always fun. But
why am I still fascinated? I think it's because when
I lived in Oakland as a very small child, the train
went right in front of our house. The engine whistle
would blow so loud. I was practically frightened
to death by this tremendous, noisy, dirty thing.

? *And the bicycles which appear over and over in your paintings? Surely you weren't frightened by a bicycle?*

a I did have a bicycle in Hong Kong and I painted it white. It really almost killed me. I remember once I was going down a hill and I didn't know how to stop.

? *It sounds pat to say that you paint a thing because it made an impression on you as a child. Were there many more things that impressed you when you were young that aren't in the paintings?*

a I really use the things like locomotives and bicycles because they are decorative and do something for me in the pictures. Of course they have a personal meaning. But you can't say of an artist he was frightened by red so he always paints in green.

? *I notice that more often than not the symbols don't fit logically into the scene. Why do your locomotives turn up in the most improbable places?*

a That's right. I use the symbols for my own purposes. For instance, I use a group of birds flying through space to get movement into my pictures. But birds are not everywhere. There's no logic to where I put them.

? *Have symbols always been important to your painting?*

a I probably use more now than I did. But I was always playing with design and color. It has been a gradual evolution and I must go on from here.

? *Your paintings are peopled with odd little men and women who are always sitting with their backs to us. Why don't they show their faces?*

a If you paint people from the back you don't disturb them.

? *They puzzle me. How can I know what they're thinking if I can't see them? I want to know what they look like.*

a That's the whole point. I want you to wonder what they are thinking and if they have one eye or two. I want you to use your imagination on the picture, be provoked by it.

129

? *I can see the faces of the cows you paint so frequently, but I wonder—what's the symbolism here?*

a I think cows are very amusing animals. Also, I like to have a big figure in my paintings. As a small man I am impressed by people and things that are large. Cows are very large animals.

Dong Kingman

? *I get the impression that you don't like to talk about what these symbols do mean to you. Am I right?*

a The mystery must remain. If I talk about them too much, then there is nothing left for me to express. I might talk them to death. I use them in a rather unconscious way. They feel right to me. But if using them became mechanical, they wouldn't belong in my pictures.

? *You don't seem to be very interested in realism although the objects in your paintings are clearly recognizable as trees or cows or whatever.*

a My forte is not realism but fantasy and humor.

? *Would you consider yourself a surrealist?*

a Most artists are surrealists. They are always dreaming something and then they paint it.

? *What would be a typical surrealist touch in your work?*

a Maybe three men riding a white bicycle which has only one wheel. I guess that is surrealist.

? *You're not a surrealist, or at least you don't belong to the surrealist school. And you have not been attracted to abstract or nonobjective painting. Could you tell me why you have steered away from what seems to be in vogue at the moment?*

a I think we should be clear about the difference between abstract painting and nonobjective painting. There is no subject at all in nonobjective painting, nothing that is recognizable as an object. Although abstract painters are concerned primarily with shapes and forms and rhythms, they may create something that suggests an object to the person who looks at their pictures.

? *Do you like nonobjective art?*

a Sooner or later I find myself in disagreement with nonobjective painting. I think they have gone too far.

? *Do you feel the same way about abstract painting?*

a Chinese painting is really abstract in its emphasis on forms, shapes, and rhythms. All modern painters are influenced by Chinese painting.

? *You are, then, a painter who does not follow any school?*

a All my art is based on design, and design is abstract. People often turn my pictures upside down to see the color and design and be able to ignore the subjects in the painting. In that sense I suppose I am an abstract painter.

Of course you are bound to fall into a style which is recognizable to people. You really can't help it. People will say that one figure in a picture reminds them of Seurat, or a tree you have drawn looks so oriental. But I have worked out my own style and it is right for me. I owe a great deal to other painters in other generations. But I don't like the idea of belonging to a school and just following other painters. I do think in abstract terms when I paint, but that doesn't make me an abstract painter. I don't like to be labeled, although many people call me a member of the "middle of the road" school.

? *What do you try to share, through your painting, of human experience? Do your paintings have a "message"?*

a Painting makes me happy and I want the people who look at my work to feel happy, too. Some of my pictures are whimsical and full of irony (people tell me). Lots of different kinds of people enjoy them and this pleases me. I don't know if my paintings have a "message." I want to express something, say something, but I also want to make the best use of the object I am painting in a purely design kind of way. If the painting comes off and gives people pleasure, I have achieved my goal. I usually say I paint "for fun," but that doesn't express anything. I only know that I have this urge to paint. When I paint I feel relaxed. I am happy. If I don't paint, then I am unhappy.

13

DORIS LEE

**22 famous
painters
and
illustrators
tell how
they work**

Photograph of the artist

The work of Doris Lee, who has been called this country's "foremost woman painter," hangs in leading museums, including the Museum of Modern Art, the Chicago Art Institute, and the Metropolitan Museum. Her fresh, pure style has brought her hundreds of magazine and advertising commissions. In addition she has illustrated a dozen or more books. Born in Aledo, Illinois, Doris Lee graduated from Ferry Hall School in Lake Forest, Illinois, and from Rockland College, Rockford, Illinois. Following her college graduation in 1927, she studied in France and Italy and at the California School of Fine Arts in San Francisco. Married to artist Arnold Blanch, she spends summers in Woodstock, New York, and winters in Key West, Florida. Doris Lee has taught in many art centers, including the Colorado Springs Fine Art Center, Michigan State College, and Florida Gulf Coast Art Center. She has also served as the President of the Woodstock Art Association. With Arnold Blanch she co-authored *Painting for Enjoyment*.

Rhythm and Pattern

I am not a primitive. I am very conscious of what I am doing. Real primitives are rare. They are untrained and they paint spontaneously and with great honesty, the way Grandma Moses did. They are genuine innocents. They often tend to paint the same subject over and over. I am constantly experimenting. I like primitives, but I like realistic or abstract painting, too. I have catholic taste. So many artists crowd my mind. The Pompeii frescoes. Byzantine mosaics. Ingres. Matisse is a great favorite. I think painters should read and listen to music as well as look at art. It reminds you of what is important to do. I like modern music, Bartok and Ives. I like poetry. Emily Dickinson, Gertrude Stein, Edith Sitwell, and Japanese poetry.

? *When magazines and advertising agencies commission you to do a painting, do they always ask you for one with a primitive flavor, a so-called "genre" scene?*

a Unfortunately, yes. I do many other kinds of work. But some of my paintings have been reproduced so widely that many people associate me exclusively with "Thanksgiving Day" or "Country Wedding." What art directors often want is a repetition of these paintings. (One of my troubles is that "yes" is a very natural word for me to say.) Some of these qualities

The Sleigh. Oil. Abbott Laboratories

will probably persist in my work, but I like exploring other media and other subjects—the theater and dance for instance. Gouache is a wonderful medium, excellent for a student to use. It dries quickly and gives you a lot of freedom. I wish I could settle down to one medium, like water color, or paint just one subject. It's perhaps a fault that I've done so many different things—movies, murals, costume design. But I do think that changing to a different medium stimulates your facility in another medium. I like oil best. After I have done gouache for a while, I come back to oil with fresh ideas on how to use it.

? *Looking at your early work it is obvious that the generally accepted traditions and principles of form and volume and depth were important to you. Your women had round arms, for example. Now they have flat ones. Why have you reduced the accepted principles of form to more two-dimensional effects? Frequently, in your work at the present time, you ignore the accepted principles of depth in perspective. While we assume this is for the sake of design, can you explain it in your own words?*

134

a There's no point in breaking up a form to make it into a golf ball or tube if you don't want to. The way you paint the edge of an object can give form. Depending upon your brush stroke you can make something advance or go back. Van Gogh's work is sometimes flat, but then sometimes he paints round. There are so many different kinds of space. It depends upon how you want your forms to relate. Different people have different ideas about perspective. The traditional Chinese painter, for example, has a very different idea from the Western traditional painter. The work tends to be more stylized, less three-dimensional.

Doris Lee

? *Very often you seem to eliminate one of the primary colors in your pictures. Can you explain why you do this?*

a I like close color relationships. It is a personal taste. I get an emotional feeling of being saturated with color, and I think it gives oneness to a painting. Right now I'm on a yellow streak. But I'm very fond of the green Picasso still life and Matisse's "Red Interior" which hang at the Museum of Modern Art in New York.

? *Your pictures are remarkable for their inner rhythm. Do you work to achieve this effect?*

a Rhythm is very important to me. I try to plan my pictures so that the eye travels over and around the elements in a way that is physically pleasurable. You feel part of the picture. You are transported in the same way as when you watch someone dance. I used to watch people look at the "Mona Lisa," and as they watched, their lips would begin to curl into a little smile. This is empathy. I want people to participate in my paintings, to feel the rhythm, to have an emotional response to them.

? *Surely, all these art forms you have tried, and succeeded at, express one dominant theme. There must be something they all have in common, even though the textures are so different and the subject matter so widely varied. What is it?*

a I'm told it looks like it all came from the same person. Like handwriting, it's my own. I don't believe the basic content changes very much in any painter's work.

135

Thanksgiving Day. Oil. The Art Institute of Chicago

? *Even though you admire the untaught, or self-taught, primitive painters, don't you think that students of art should learn the basic principles and techniques of the craft?*

a Oh, yes. If I were going to school today, I would want a very solid and fine training in drawing. That would be a very fine thing to have, because young people eventually feel frustrated without it. I had a lot of drawing when I was starting out. I majored in philosophy in college, but I took painting as my minor. I studied in Paris, going to school all day. I haunted the museums. I studied at the Kansas City Art Institute and the California School of Fine Arts. Another thing you must develop is self-discipline. Artists do like freedom. That's one reason they want to be artists. They think they will be able to do as they please, but art is very demanding.

An artist has to know how to handle a lot of things. If he doesn't learn them, the lack will bother him later on. You have to know how to control your hands so that you can draw the way you feel. You have to know how to mix paints. These are technical things which artists have known for centuries. You should learn so that you won't be in awe of them or fear them. You can discard them later if you wish to do so.

Doris Lee

? *Could you recall the procedure that seems most natural to you in making a painting? What do you usually do?*

a First, you look at the subject and are a little contemplative, appreciating it, thinking of its color and shapes. You may make a few quick sketches for reference later on. You work in stages. I like to make little drawings before I begin the picture. If I make a big drawing, I lose simplicity and impact. It is better to make the drawings small and not too detailed. If you want to remember detail you can make another drawing to show texture, for example. I don't want the sketches to dictate to me because the picture will develop as I begin to paint, and it will often turn into something I hadn't counted on in the beginning.

I sometimes put charcoal marks on the canvas as an indication of the forms. But sometimes I don't. You don't always work alike. You approach painting in different ways. I think it's wonderful if you can be deliberate about planning a painting. When I get a deliberate streak I'm very definite. But often you have to paint out the very thing you started the picture about. You have to be able to do this without feeling grieved. In painting you have a lot of casualties. You cannot be fearful. I don't think I "see" the final painting before I start. The minute you put anything down you must make the next element relate to the first. It's always a surprise—sometimes a shock or a pleasure. I think I paint best when I am completely relaxed and the picture just develops. My best pictures were the easiest ones to paint.

Whenever you see anything that excites you, the response is emotional. You shouldn't be critical or intellectual when you start a picture. You get more critical as you get into it—and then very critical when you finish.

When you're creating the picture, there's the excitement of putting colors together, or creating the shapes and forms. I see a flower growing in a certain way in the garden. I come in and make a little drawing of it. I'm still excited by what I've seen.

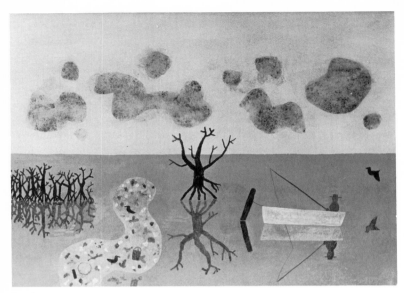

Off Shore. Gouache

Then, when I'm actually constructing the painting, it's a combination of emotional and intellectual activity. You're in action when you're making a picture, and all you know and feel about art comes into play. The hard thing in painting is to get the forms and colors going together.

? *You once said that "fear of making a mistake is the greatest mistake a painter can make." Can you throw out a picture that doesn't satisfy you?*

a If it's hopeless, I can. But by putting it away for a while I can get a new approach to it. When I get it out again, I can sometimes make it work. If a painting isn't working at all, I think you should block it out completely. The act of destruction helps you start over. It is just as important to make failures as it is to make successes. You learn a lot from failures.

It doesn't bother me when people don't like or don't understand my work. I'm used to it. You have to believe in what you're doing. I've had letters asking me why I did this or that. People will say to me, "Doris, you paint such nice little people. Why do you want to paint those great big forms?" It isn't

138

Doris Lee

important to me whether they like it or not. Like everyone, artists need some appreciation, but it is fatal to try to please and not paint naturally. An artist doesn't expect everyone to love him. After all, he has the freedom to do what he wants to do most— make pictures. I started to paint because I wanted to make something. The whole fascination now with painting is to see what I can make. As an artist, you are free to make what you want. This is probably why most people paint. Art supplies something that life doesn't. It gives me an enormous appreciation of how things look, a beautiful and sensuous feeling of the texture and rhythm of nature.

I love the country. It smells good. The country isn't as rigid as the city. I feel like painting here in Woodstock. There is so much in the garden to paint, from bugs to leaves. When I am in Key West in the winter, I get fascinated with things in the water.

I just like painting that is rather simple, without pretense. I suppose I do create this effect deliberately, but I am expressing my feelings about nature at the same time. When you paint, you would like to have people see the purity of things, the things you feel. But I don't believe that at the time of painting you think of communication. You are so involved with making something and seeing how it comes out that your principal concern is to enjoy yourself and interest yourself and worry yourself.

? *You have said that a painting must have "mystery, oneness, and a sense of authority." What do you mean by this?*

a I don't mean that a painter should try to puzzle people. But every good picture has to have some mystery, because that's the way the world is and the way we are. A picture should have a unified mood or impact, however complicated it is. As long as the colors make patterns together and the forms fit into the general theme, you can achieve oneness. You may have thirty people in a painting, but you must work so the result is that of one picture and not thirty pictures put together. It should be a unified experience to look at a picture.

I'm not sure now if authority is the right word. I mean conviction, really, a genuine feeling, forthrightness. I think a good picture should surely express an attitude or personality. If it does this, we shouldn't worry about what school of painting it represents or how important the painter is.

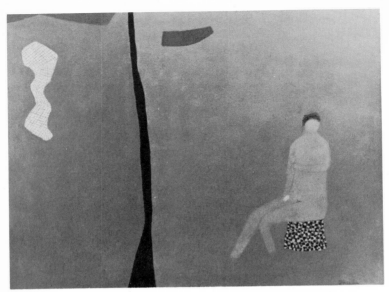

Bather. Oil

? *Is it as rewarding to you to interpret other people's
ideas as it is to paint a completely personal
expression? Or do you paint as you like even though
on an advertising or editorial assignment you are
involved with the client's wishes?*

a I like to take a commission if it is something I can do
and like to do. If I have the freedom to do as good a
job as I can, then I don't mind whatever restrictions
there are as to size, color, etc. In France, all the
leading artists, Miro and Chagall and others, do
commercial work. I recently accepted a commission to
do a painting for a Christmas card. They liked the
picture, but they wondered if I would mind lightening
the sky. I had made it a deep red. In thinking it
over I decided the sky would have been better in that
curious green you get in winter. I didn't mind
changing it because it didn't involve a change in the
spirit of the painting. A good art director should not
try to change the style of a painter. I refuse all
commissions unless I feel that they are very right for
me. If it is right, I enjoy doing the work.

All artists must face and solve problems in painting.
One form relates to another. To get things to fit
together and work them out is often complex. I like to
140 work puzzles and I like mathematics. I often take

problems to bed with me to solve, the way other people read themselves to sleep with mysteries.

? *What kind of subject should the student painter choose? How can he tell if it is worth painting?*

Doris Lee

a By painting it. No, seriously, some of the most improbable subjects turn out to be exciting. Students are always asking, "Do you think I have enough talent to go on?" Nobody can know until he "goes on." You don't know what you are capable of until it is painted. And you don't know the possibilities in a subject until you have explored them. I know people feel a little helpless when they start a painting. I think they should start with what they like best. As I've mentioned, I like nature. Other people may like boats or cities. I knew a woman once who painted a remarkable picture of her sewing basket because she liked sewing. There is plenty to paint if you look for it.

The important thing is to learn how to see. You must learn this just as a musician must learn to hear. Study painting and go to museums. This, combined with your own drawing, will help you learn to see. If you could help teach people how to see—and be—they would have fewer problems as artists.

When I see something that moves me—however fragmentary an impression it is—I put it down immediately while it is still vivid in my mind. I like to examine things close up. When you look closely at a shell or a flower you notice the interesting textural quality, and associations then come to you.

? *You aren't trying to achieve an exact reproduction of nature in our paintings, are you?*

a I certainly don't copy nature. You can best express the authentic character of a thing by concentrating on the shape in your imagination rather than on the exact appearance before you. When you have trouble with a painting it is usually because you are paying too much attention to the literal appearance and not enough to the over-all shape. You must also be selective when it comes to color. Usually I eliminate at least one of the primary colors. Actually light does something of the same thing in nature; if reds are bright in the light greens are not. Taking away some colors and concentrating on one or two gives a pleasant kind of understatement. Hold on to your own way of sensing things. Every one of us reacts to nature in a different way. But try to sharpen your powers of observation.

141

14

FRED LUDEKENS

**22 famous
painters
and
illustrators
tell how
they work**

Photograph of the artist

Fred Ludekens is in the unique, and enviable, position of a working artist who knows the problems of the advertiser from all possible angles. An advertising executive, he is also a veteran illustrator. He has enjoyed both sides of his double-barreled career. "I like pictures that have problems in them to solve. I like the intellectual workout it gives me." Born in California, Ludekens grew up in Canada, where his family moved when his father died. Ludekens was fond of drawing as a boy but, undecided about art as a career, he went to work for an advertising agency in San Francisco, and attended school part time.

Ludekens studied art under Otis Shepard in the University of California Extension School but did not submit a drawing until the last day of the class. Then he brought in his first assignment and Shepard praised it highly. Until that moment Ludekens was not sure that he had enough skill to become a commercial artist. With new confidence he decided to free-lance in art. Eventually he worked for the Lord and Thomas advertising agency as art director of the San Francisco office. He later became co-creative director of Foote, Cone and Belding.

Paralleling an outstanding career as an advertising art executive and artist is Ludekens' editorial work. He has illustrated books and magazine serials and is sought after in both advertising and editorial art circles. Fred Ludekens is still doing work for accounts he handled years ago. This is proof indeed that he has always been able to give the client what he wants— and, in fact, improve upon the original concept of the assignment.

The Changing Art Market

I believe the basic picture requirement is *clarity*, and simultaneously, the right content. Clarity and content are synonymous. It little matters how beautiful, compelling, and interesting the surface of a picture might be if it does not say the right thing and say it clearly.

The volume of advertising is tremendous. The differences in most products are minute. *Attention* is a major problem. Anytime you can "write copy" in a picture using three quarters of the space—or in television clearly demonstrate or explain the idea visually—you are way ahead. You get attention and you get it centered right on the idea. This takes illustration beyond its role of illustrating words. It becomes a language in itself. It can, however, only

Lesser Snow Geese. Water color. *True, The Man's Magazine*

be "successful" if the picture maker is sympathetic, knowledgeable, and objective in his thinking in order to fulfill the requirements of the problem. He is interested primarily in communicating to his audience, clearly and convincingly, the promise and benefit of the idea. The means by which he does it *should always be planned to do only this,* not to dilute the idea.

? *What, in your opinion, is the value of the picture to the total creative effort in advertising?*

a Offhand, I would say it is the instant communication of the idea. In advertising, the picture should be good copy. I believe it should do more than illustrate. It should appeal to the mind and have something to say of substance and meaning. Often, text is written describing the picture, usually saying what the picture has already said. In advertising, I think the picture has a job to do, and the text should only say what the picture cannot say—the reason, the benefit, the price, and so on.

? *What contribution does a good illustration make to an advertisement?*

a *Content!* Content is what you are drawing, not how you draw. At this time we seem to be on a "technique jag" which gets in the way of clear communication.

144

**? ** *How much of the fundamental copy job rests on the shoulders of the picture?*

a As much as possible. I believe the right picture can be very clear and convincing in setting up the sales proposition and interesting people. For the average product little text is necessary. People in advertising are basically copy minded, and their idea of a picture is something to illustrate their words. A good picture man with advertising sense can make an outstanding contribution to advertising.

Fred Ludekens

**? ** *What trends have most influenced illustration in the last thirty years?*

a I believe contemporary painting has had influence in illustration, especially recently. The technique of modern art is contagious and so it gets mixed up with business. I think the illustrator's effort now is to be "different." I question the understanding of the public of this differentness. There is nothing wrong with modern art. But it is personal and quite restricted in audience. It seems to me the illustrator's job in business and publishing is to reach the public clearly.

**? ** *How would you describe the meshing of the artist's talent and the client's needs when an advertising illustration is being created?*

a The mechanics are such in advertising that the responsibilities are in the hands of copy and art people. Often, the illustrator's contribution is so controlled it is not all that it should be. In my opinion, the ideal way is for art director, copy writer, and illustrator to have a serious discussion as to how the picture problem can best be solved *before* the advertisement has been decided and sketched by an art director and submitted to a client. Unfortunately for the illustrator, the procedure is usually the reverse of this.

**? ** *You feel then that the person who makes the picture would make more of a contribution if he were included in the early planning sessions?*

a Yes, I do. But this is very difficult because of the structural setup of the advertising business. There is no provision in the structure for "outside" people to get in at the planning and concept stage and make the

A Town Named Hate. Brush and felt pen.
Reprinted by special permission of *The Saturday Evening Post.*
© 1961 The Curtis Publishing Company

contribution many of them could make. A few years ago, I was fortunate in being able to do this for a large advertiser with positive success, but it took a real all-out effort.

? *What, in your opinion, are the three most important qualities a successful illustrator must have?*

a You must know these three things:
How to draw—if you cannot draw, you restrict what you can say.
What to draw—if you do not know what to draw, you won't say anything.
Who the Audience is—if you don't consider who you're talking to and consider what they understand, you won't reach them.
The whole idea is to "talk to people" visually.

? *What essential training must the illustrator bring to the job?*

a Assuming he has talent, likes to draw and paint, the most important thing for him to have is a knowledge of the business he is in. Most illustrators know very little about business or writing. They just like to make pictures. This isn't enough. They should know what the picture is *specifically* required to do and why. They must be interested in the why and make an all-out effort to make the picture work. This is what they are being paid to do.

? If an illustrator develops a distinct style, how does this help (and sometimes hurt) his career?

Fred Ludekens

a A distinct style is all right *if* you have a fluid and alert mind. Pictures all ought to solve communication problems in a certain way. If the style becomes more important than the problem solution, the illustrator obviously has failed. Often, a distinct style does not properly fit the problem and often, a distinct style is only a fad of differentness and is junked when a "fresh new style" comes along. To be concerned only with manner is superficial. I do not believe this is a business of being different. It is a business of being *right* to the right people at the right time.

? Why did you choose art as a career?

a Because I like to make pictures.

? Must an artist have talent?

a Yes. Most children have talent and like to make pictures. It's a desire to record what they see. It's a desire to say something. I believe talent is fundamentally a desire. If the desire is strong and compelling, the talent develops. To learn to draw and paint is hard and to do so, the desire must be strong enough for the artist to go through the effort of development.

? What kind of training did you have?

a None. If there is such a thing, I am self-taught. I had a strong desire to make pictures. My talent was limited. I simply developed it as best I could by plain hard work.

? Was there a turning point in your career?

a I don't think there was a turning point. I just climbed the long ladder one rung at a time. I married young and had to make a living. I felt I could be a successful artist if I could make saleable pictures. I did. The career developed. At the time you were supposed to learn how to draw. No one I knew drew

Thames Estuary. Opaque water color. *True, The Man's Magazine*

from photos. You thought it out and drew it. You learned to study objects and people and to transpose what you saw into pictures. Experience taught me the requirements. I formed very objective opinions, as you can tell by the answers to these questions. And I have lived by them. This is hard work, but I survived.

? *You said, and I quote, "You make your own luck. Timing does it, so don't get ahead of yourself." Can you explain further?*

**Fred
Ludekens**

a I guess I mean you don't get many chances to be
wrong. To use a familiar term an illustrator is only as
good as his last job. Now that is not quite true but
pretty close. In my opinion many young artists make
a mistake by trying to get the big jobs before they are
really ready for them. One job hardly counts unless it
will produce another. The immature artist, if he fails,
seldom gets another chance with the same publisher.
With limited good outlets for illustration this is
hardly something he can afford. Doing well means
good selection and interpretation of the manuscript's
most effective illustrative possibilities. Two
fundamentals are necessary. First, to know what an
effective illustrative situation really is. Second, the
ability to draw it, regardless of the subject, its
complication, its simplicity, or the time required to
do it well. Without this approach the illustrator's
chance of success over a period of time is doubtful.
An illustrator never knows what he may be required
to do on his next assignment. His experience as a keen
observer, a person of broad experience in travel, work,
sports and so on helps him bring *his* understanding
and feeling to the job. This is a requisite to success.

? *You have also said, "If you plant the seeds and the
trees grow tall enough someone will see them." What
did you mean?*

a I'll try to explain it. Many years ago I illustrated
a book of yarns written by one of my friends. I did
twenty-two full-page pictures and twenty-one small
chapter headings, designed the hard cover and did the
jacket in full color for a total sum of just three
hundred and fifty dollars. This started me on my
career as a fiction illustrator. Here I believe "the trees
grew tall enough to see." Directly from this group of
illustrations I received an unsolicited assignment to
do an eight-part serial for the Curtis Publishing
Company. This was important in numerous ways,
and was directly responsible for many years of good
assignments on varied subjects. *Good* assignments
allow an illustrator to demonstrate his consistent
ability to handle effectively a wide variety of subject
matter which in turn furthers his experiences and
broadens and extends his career. A career isn't a career
unless it lasts. An illustrator isn't an illustrator unless
he's illustrating. It takes years to get the right
opportunity. Recognize its value and its hazards.
Don't throw it away.

Horses. Opaque water color.
Reprinted by special permission of *The Saturday Evening Post.*
© 1949 The Curtis Publishing Company

? *What illustrators influenced you most as a young artist?*

a When I started, Harvey Dunn, Dean Cornwell, Pruett Carter, Walter Biggs, Henry Raleigh, John LaGatta, Frank Hoffman, and Gruger were the major illustrators. This was in the twenties. They influenced every young illustrator. How much I was influenced, others can tell better than I. I think all of them influenced me in different ways.

? *How did your style develop?*

a I really think it developed as I solved printing and mechanical problems.

? *How important is originality?*

a I think you have to be yourself. Originality is not a specific term. I feel you have to rest your case on how *you* think. If you think well, you'll make it. If you are not progressing, you better reevaluate yourself. Don't complain about the world being wrong.

? *What does the illustrator communicate to his audience? More particularly, what do you try to communicate?*

Fred Ludekens

a I try to communicate to the best of my ability the advertising or selling requirement clearly and convincingly. In fiction illustration, I believe the success of the picture usually lies in the *selection* of what you illustrate. It should be in character and show feeling for the story and be compelling in concept and treatment. To deviate from this, I feel is to be dishonest to the reader.

? *If you were to define the single quality which a good picture possesses and a poor one does not—what would it be?*

a The right content designed to communicate the content to people, attractively, clearly, and convincingly. If it doesn't do this, it isn't working. This is the objective, and the way to achieve it is wide open to any illustrator. It depends on *you*. An illustrator, as I said before, should have more than talent. A few brains, understanding, and judgment also help. These are required to make successful pictures.

? *How carefully do you plan a picture? Is your response to a subject emotional, intellectual, or a combination of the two?*

a Very carefully. I believe composition is the most forceful part of a picture. I try to make a cohesive whole out of many elements—the idea, mood, action, arrangement, color, and so on—as *I* interpret the problem. If I am illustrating a piece of fiction, I believe my response is emotional, influenced some by my awareness of the audience and the publisher. On nonfiction, I believe my response is just the reverse.

? *What satisfaction have you gotten from art as a career? Can you imagine yourself in any other profession?*

a I wouldn't trade my work or do it differently if I had another try. There are problems of self discipline, control of work, the kind of work, and so on, but, all in all, the illustrator is "out of sight" and can pretty well control his time and energy. I have managed to do so.

15

FLETCHER MARTIN

**22 famous
painters
and
illustrators
tell how
they work**

Photograph of the artist

It has been said of Fletcher Martin that "he has an amazing knack for stopping down action at its top speed." His paintings of prize fighters, cowboys, and bullfights suggest immediacy and reflect the perceptive eye of one who has seen at first hand what he paints. Martin's early life as harvester, lumberjack, boxer, and sailor gave him an enviable background as a painter of action scenes. Born in Palisade, Colorado, Martin learned the printing trade as a boy and then joined the U.S. Navy when he was eighteen. Until 1935 he worked as a printer and painted in his free time. His first museum-sponsored one-man show was held at the San Diego Fine Arts Gallery in 1934. Subsequently, his work has been shown at the Museum of Modern Art, the Carnegie Institute, the Corcoran Museum, the Metropolitan Museum, the National Academy, the Pennsylvania Academy, and at important national exhibitions. He has had twenty-five one-man shows in museums and galleries in the United States, and his work has been sent abroad for view in traveling exhibitions. Martin was an artist war correspondent for *Life* Magazine in 1943-44. He is known for his magazine illustrations as well as his fine arts painting and has won awards and prizes from the Art Directors Clubs of New York and Chicago. Although he never attended art school, Martin succeeded both Grant Wood, as Artist-in-Residence at the University of Iowa, and Thomas Hart Benton, at the Kansas City Art Institute. He has taught at many other art schools and universities. He lives in Woodstock, New York.

**Action
in
Painting**

It would be good to have a complicated reason for being an artist. I could have been much more solvent doing something else. Being an artist has been a difficult thing, but I paint because it has been my major interest ever since I can remember. I never even thought of being anything else but an artist. As a kid, I didn't know exactly what I wanted to be, but there was awareness that I was longing for something. Art satisfied that longing.

Nothing is as valuable as the privilege of painting but, at the same time, I don't deny a certain, maybe contemptible, but human pleasure in recognition. However, if painting didn't carry me as far as making my living goes, I would work at some other job, but I would continue to paint as much as my energy would allow. It's necessary and I love it.

Country Dance. Oil

? *From your long experience painting sports and action, would you say that this subject matter demands certain skills of the artist? Surely figure drawing is important here.*

a Of course you have to be able to draw well. You can't fake the human figure because the body tension is part of the drama. The problem of a sports painting is to make the tension convincing both in terms of the drawing and the sport itself. Too often there is just a depiction, no real translation of the sports event into aesthetic terms. Nearly all sports paintings are

Fletcher
Martin

pretty bad, really. I mean to say, the subject hasn't
been handled well. I don't mean to criticize other
painters, but to do a good painting of a sports event
you need to understand it. An example is the
bullfight. Many artists are fascinated by the
bullfight. They depict the thing, but the part that
appeals to them may be the worst part of the fight.
Their choice would make an aficionado laugh.
I understand what the show is, what the conflict is,
what the drama should be. To make an action picture,
you need to feel the action. I have seen hundreds of
fights. I often go to Mexico even now just to see
them. I think the bullfight is the most spectacular
of all sports because it is a pageant and not really a
contest. Boxing is exciting, too, of course. Each
sport has its own particular interest. That's what
makes sports so diverse and challenging to the painter.

? *Although you have painted many other subjects, do
you think the sports paintings, for which you are most
known, represent your work at its best?*

a There was a period when I did a lot of fight things—
bullfights and prizefights. At this time, I was
getting a great deal of attention as a new artist.
When magazines wrote about me, they tended to
identify me as "the guy who does sports." At the time
I succeeded Grant Wood at Iowa, *Life* described me
as an ex-sailor, ex-fighter, who had turned painter.
This kind of myth fits my appearance. I don't mean to
say it's totally inaccurate. I am very much interested in
sports, but I like to paint other things as well.
George Bellows' name, for example, is synonymous
with boxing, and again with him it was just a
circumstance. He happened to do the Dempsey-Firpo
thing, but he also did every other kind of subject. He
painted more female portraits, by far, than boxing
scenes. I've done ten females to every sports picture.
The female figure just interests me. Whether it was
erotic or not in the beginning, I don't know.

? *The most diverse subjects, then, can stimulate an
artist?*

a You can make a hell of a painting about anything, but
it is absolutely essential that it interest you. The
more interested you are the better, provided your
intent is aesthetic and not just sentimental. When
sentimentality permeates the picture, it fails. I've
got nothing against sunsets, for example, but

Bullfight. Oil. Butler Institute of American Art, Youngstown, Ohio

I wouldn't paint one. It doesn't interest me as a
subject for painting. It interests me as a sunset.
Most landscapes I've done were done because I wanted
to be out in the open air. I enjoy it. Whetting the
faculties of observation is very important.
I recommend it. But for me, landscape painting
doesn't hold the excitement that figure painting does.
The painter must be objective about his work. What
I'm saying presupposes the ability to do what you
want to do. Assuming you have the technical ability to
make a statement, I would say that even if the
motivation is sentimental or sentimentally nostalgic,
once this motivation brings you to the canvas, you
should try to have as objective an attitude as possible.

?   *What do you and other artists mean by "a statement"?*

a   I mean aesthetic statement. The statement you make
on the canvas is what you are. It should be all of a
piece. Picasso has been the most published artist of
our generation and one of the most versatile.
Whatever eccentricities he has indulged in, there is
still an underlying principle in all his work. It
represents Picasso the man. Your abilities as an artist
help you make the statement that you, as a man,
would like to make. You may be motivated by all sorts

156

of impulses to make the picture, but when you get into the studio before the canvas, you must be totally objective. In organizing the picture you should try to think of it in terms of texture, drawing, order, elimination. The greatest virtue a student can have is the ability to eliminate the unnecessary. A sort of grab-bag thing is nearly always a bad painting. The stuff that makes a painting good is the competence of the painter, not his sentimental involvement with the subject matter.

Fletcher Martin

? *But shouldn't he sustain some emotional feeling for his subject while he is making the picture?*

a My answer may sound like a contradiction, but it isn't really a contradiction. Instead of sentimental involvement, the painter should have an empathetic involvement. In painting a prizefight, for example, he would need to know what it feels like to fight. Before you can draw and order a thing, you need to get the feel of it. Good pictures come out of one's experience, out of one's life, even though the symbol of this experience—the subject of the picture—may be quite obscure.

? *The many paintings you have made of mother and child are remarkably realistic. Yet you certainly have never lived this role. How do you explain this?*

a To have an empathy doesn't mean that you must literally step into another person's shoes. You must understand, deeply and sympathetically, how the other person feels. I don't have to be a matador to paint bullfights. And when you understand fully, you can be discriminating. The tourist who has never seen a bullfight before may respond only to the blood. The good things in a bullfight are the subtle relationships between the beast and the man. This is why the sport is exciting. A person could make a career of painting this one subject. It is formal, diverse, more like the theater than sport.

What I may be trying to do is to make something that will communicate my interest or my excitement in a particular painting. A really good painting, a fresh painting, should be of interest even if a person doesn't like the subject. People say, "I don't like this because I don't like bullfights." A painting should be judged on how well it is made, its visual impact. The subject is incidental.

Lullaby. Oil. Collection of Mr. and Mrs. Clifford D. West

? *You were largely self-taught. Can you tell us how you mastered the fundamentals of art while supporting yourself?*

a I drew all the time. I associated with painters.
I was grown up before I ever saw a museum or gallery. Nobody could have been less informed than I was, but once I did discover something about the world of art, I was very diligent about finding out all I could. I did this by studying on my own, and I would go to free night classes in figure drawing. If your curiosity is great enough, even about a highly specialized profession, you can become educated. If you want an education very much, you can get it. If I could do it over, I would go to art school or take our course. I wasn't able to as a young man. I was going to sea or making a living.

The student painter should know his trade. He should have the ability to handle the materials, organize the space. Once this is achieved, he can have the *pride* that comes with craftsmanship. Of course, reaching this point also invites ten thousand more complex and subtle problems. The idea that you learn to do it and then you're all set is nonsense if you're a serious person. You may live to be a thousand years old and still run into roadblocks. The student has to be discouraged from avoiding the modest problems. Right off the bat he hopes to do the masterpiece, and he doesn't even know how to begin. He should understand that he cannot be a competent artist until he learns his trade. He should draw all the time. He should regard his work as a marvelous objective and take the appropriate modest pleasure in doing it. He should aspire to a high degree of professionalism.

Fletcher Martin

? *Do you know how the picture is going to be resolved before you actually begin to work on it?*

a I find the painting while doing it. The basic conception is usually a felt thing. Then it must be established. I sometimes make drawings, many drawings of the subject I'm going to do, in order to find the attitudes that will work. I have an idea about the order of the picture, but in the course of making it, many changes occur. One should always be willing to make changes. However proud one is of any painting, it should be expendable. One should work on the whole picture—and every day. One shouldn't get too involved with any particular detail or live in the occurrence depicted. The picture itself is an object. You can get the image—something that resembles the subject—in fifteen minutes. The final clarity of the painting, however, is the sum of many decisions that have little to do with literal representation. It is the addition of all the small refinements that gives the picture its quality.

? *Is there a set pattern in the way you work?*

a Everybody works in a different way. There have been people like Grant Wood, who have been very deliberate. He would make a diagrammatic study of his painting, working on it for three months before he actually began to paint. I don't do that. I feel there are several alternatives to the order of the painting. This is something you have to investigate. I make a lot of drawings, but I don't necessarily make a lot for every picture. When I approach the painting, I never begin with a fixed idea of how the painting will look. I know the statement I want to make and, as I said before, I find the painting while doing it. The solution that works may be achieved on the last day. Often I paint the whole thing over every day.

? *Do you ever use a camera to capture action, or a model, and then refer to the photograph as you work?*

a I don't ordinarily use a camera, although I have done so on field assignments. I took a camera to Normandy,

Whither Ulysses. Oil. Private Collection

but I discovered that my own sketches were much
more useful. I discovered that what your eye gives you
and what your heart responds to is all-important. If
you can draw it on the spot, you can draw it later. Even
the most cursory note does tend to fix the image and
help one to the point where total recall is automatic.
When I go through the material I have gathered on a
trip and pick up any sketch at random, I can feel the
weather, smell the smells, hear the sounds that were
there because I made it, no matter how long ago. It is
real to me because I lived there a little while, maybe
a minute, maybe an hour, but intensely. None of the
photos I have taken has that power. It is because they
are too explicit, and the making of the shot did not
involve me as the sketch did.

Fletcher Martin

Drawing is very important to the total realization of the painting. But you shouldn't think that every drawing you do is precious. A person should draw all the time, much the way he eats and sleeps. Every day I draw, and it doesn't have to be a drawing *for* something. One's powers of observation should be made as acute as possible so that anything you understand you can get down without having the subject right in front of you. The tyranny of the model is a terrible thing. I know very able people whose habits have been so developed they don't think about drawing without having something to look at. It is a tremendously hampering thing to do. When you understand the human figure, you can draw the figure. You don't need a model.

? *What do you think is the value of experimental art?*

a Every picture is experimental. And that's one of the main reasons why painting is so exciting. When I look at a painting, I look for an experience. People who say, "I like it, but I wouldn't want to hang it on my wall," usually mean that a picture disturbs them. It's too violent. They think pictures should have sobriety. Well, I've seen a lot of sober pictures I wouldn't hang for that very reason. There are people who may not like some of the nonrepresentational work. There is plenty of bad representational work around, too. The ratio of good to bad in both schools is about the same. Nonobjective painting has patterns that mean something. If they are excellently arranged, the picture works. I personally don't want to paint that way, but many of my friends and contemporaries do, and I can respond to their work. I'm certainly not going to go out and do it, because it isn't my way, my feeling. I don't criticize anybody for painting the way he wants to as long as it is a true thing for him. I've had students who did something imitative of a very important painter, and it was lousy and weak, I would ask them, "What are you intending to do here?" and they couldn't say. All the good men, the really big men, who first started contemporary and even nonobjective art are well-trained people. They can draw like Ingres if they want to. Picasso, for example, is a superb draftsman.

? *Can an artist develop originality?*

a Originality is something you can't simply acquire. Either you have this highly prized creative thing that

makes your work original, or you don't. I think
originality is a product of maturity. Lots of students
get trapped in the effort to be original. After fifty
million paintings have been painted you can see that
it is impossible to be highly original. There is
always precedent. Who would want to be that original
anyway? A better intent is to see that one's work is
truly one's own—an honest expression of deep
personal feelings. The whole history of art, which
can't help affect one, will be filtered through your
own personality to produce a sort of original
statement.

**Fletcher
Martin**

? *What makes an artist successful?*

a First you have to decide what success is. You can be
successful and nobody has ever heard of you or you
have never been out of your studio. I think talent is a
very essential quality, but just what it is, what
shape it takes, is not so easy to define. In some
schools of painting, talent depends on how good at
conformity the painters are. For example, you are
said to have talent if you can make your drawing look
like the plaster cast. Yet the most able in copying
the cast may be the least talented as artists.
I remember one boy I knew who had been studying
for ten years. He could do the figure, male or female.
He could do the figure with the epidermis and then
skin it and draw the muscles and arteries. This was all
he could do. This had been a learned lesson and he
was dexterous with the hand, but had no talent.
Facility is often confused with talent, but they are not
the same. I've had students who were poor as artists
simply because they were so facile. Facility is
esteemed by those who don't have it, but many bad
things are bad because of the obvious facility.
Picasso deliberately seeks a clumsy sort of handling.
He avoids slickness, although you can sometimes find
it in his work.

? *Has your style changed over the years?*

a I don't think it's changed much, basically. Since I've
never been conscious of a style, I've never imitated
anybody or consciously sought a style. My abilities
have improved, I hope. I've applied them in different
ways. Style emerges out of a person's absorption in
his own problems and situation. I try to paint
directly, without any thought of other paintings, other
people's work. Of course all artists are influenced by

162

others to a degree. But some influences are not conscious, at least not with me. I think an artist who did have a tremendous effect on me was a Mexican painter with whom I worked in the early thirties named Sequeiros. Then, too, Picasso influenced me. More than anyone in my generation, he broke with style and precedent. He was an indirect influence on my attitudes.

? *You have done commissions for* Life *and* Sports Illustrated, *as well as other publications. As a fine-arts painter, did you have trouble adjusting to commercial restrictions? Or were there any?*

a There was never any problem for me because there was no art direction involved. I was not restricted. I brought in the drawings and they chose those they wanted me to develop into paintings. However, I will admit that when you are doing a commission, there is a problem, a subtle problem. You don't want to do it over six times, so you consider the person who commissioned you. Even though this kind of unconscious direction exists, and I don't deny it, this is not so difficult a supervision as what one gives oneself. I mean to say, the freedom to do what you want to do doesn't automatically produce a good thing. I don't suffer, because I enjoy the whole trial and tribulation of the problem. But a commission has a much more positive and definable goal than a painting you're just doing to please yourself. Freedom is desirable, but it can be an adversary too.

16
AL PARKER

22 famous painters and illustrators tell how they work

Photograph of the artist

Alfred Charles Parker has been illustrating stories for the major magazines of America for more than twenty-five years. He is still recognized as "the great innovator." Art directors say he never repeats himself, and they agree that he is one of the most widely imitated artists of his time. His influence on popular illustration has been pervasive. Parker was born in St. Louis. He says that before he could read he was painting faces on wooden clothes pins. He loved to draw but the only person in the family who thought he had any talent was his grandfather, Captain Charles J. Bender, a Mississippi River steamboat captain. He staked Parker to a year's tuition at the St. Louis School of Fine Arts at Washington University. Here, Parker discovered that his early talent could be directed into professional craftsmanship. As soon as he had established himself as a commercial artist with a studio of his own, Parker began sending samples of his work to New York magazines. He got assignments from the *Ladies' Home Journal, McCall's, Cosmopolitan,* and others. In 1935 he decided to move to New York, to be near the important art markets. Almost immediately he became widely sought after as an illustrator. Parker has received more than twenty-five gold medals and awards of excellence for his illustrations. Although Parker and his family now live in Carmel Valley, California, he travels here and abroad on assignments.

Innovation

I think one of the things I like best about illustration is the fact that things are always changing. It's always tomorrow. Illustration has taken a new turn, closer to the fine arts. I feel that artists are doing work that is a lot like the Impressionists. It means a great deal to be associated with these newer trends. Today, artists don't have to be so literal. Of course, you have to communicate so that the people are recognizable, but the point of view and the handling can be fresh and different. You are in competition with the photograph, so you have to put something unique into a painting, and this is the challenge.

? *Over the years there have been many Parker styles. Don't you run the risk of losing your identity as an artist when you abandon one approach for another?*

a This change is a style in itself. Developing an approach and then dropping it in favor of something

The Rich Woman. Gouache.
Reprinted by special permission of the *Ladies' Home Journal.*
© 1947 The Curtis Publishing Company

fresh is a completely calculated move on my part.

The artist should be himself above all. His own personality is what he should try to communicate. There is a great demand now, more than ever before, for individuality in art. The more you are like yourself, the better off you are. It's a great break for anyone starting out today. You aren't expected to imitate. You are expected to do something personal. Our ideas of people are changing. It used to be that you could draw only one kind of child—with blond curly hair and freckles. Thank goodness, that's not so today. Of course, you can't be too extreme. It's a human being you're drawing and the head must rest on the shoulders.

? *Do you recall a comparable period in illustration when change was this important?*

a The age-old struggle to remold the scheme of things takes place in almost every decade. The old clichés of illustration began to fade toward the end of the

1950's. New illustrators with a fresh intensity and
enthusiasm appeared around 1960 and their work
stimulated magazines to experiment. It is a question,
however, as to which came first—the magazines' quest
for something new or the young illustrators' offer of
vitality. A period of "anything goes" resulted but that
has now abated. Some illustrations of this period were
poetic, some were rugged. The dainty pretty little
things which had been favored by some illustrators
disappeared from magazine pages. So did "Kiss Me,"
lettered in lavender on candy hearts. Today the
emphasis is on the big scene, the over-all mood of the
story. The younger illustrators have begun to play a
vital role in illustration because they bring a wholly
new attitude toward it. Many have shown promise
of being true painters. Indeed some are familiar to
gallery goers already.

What was merely a glimmer of light on the
illustration scene has now loomed into a brilliant
beacon. I am speaking of the newly revived field of
documentary reportage for the illustrator. Not long
ago I covered the Grand Prix of Europe, that exciting
automobile race, for *Sports Illustrated*. How thrilling
it was to paint fact after my years of painting fiction.
My advice to the budding illustrator is this—take
advantage of this decade! Paint from deep down
inside of you. Be aware and always keep your sense
of humor.

? *But why do you work so hard not to look like Al
Parker?*

a I can't help trying new techniques. That's the fun of
it. There was a time when I seemed to be sticking my
neck out, but now everybody is sticking his neck
out and experimenting. It's a good thing, too,
because this fresh artistic attitude was long overdue.

Why not use everything available to you? You never
know when you are going to need to work in a
different medium to get the effect you want. And if
you are stuck in one rut, you can't do it easily. That's
why I think young artists should familiarize themselves
with all the media available and experiment with
them all. I once did an illustration in oils on plywood
and let the plywood show through. Another time
I used a nail punch to make the dots on a girl's dress.
These weren't stunts. I think they were legitimate and
appropriate to the problem I had to solve in these
illustrations. This kind of experimentation helps to

The Alibi. Pencil and water color.
Reprinted by special permission of the *Ladies' Home Journal.*
© 1959 The Curtis Publishing Company

keep my work fresh. But I don't believe in trickiness.
I don't think a gimmick can ever conceal the basic
inadequacies of a poor illustration. I have worked in
pencil, tempera, water color, gouache, oil, wash,
airbrush, pen and ink, dry brush, charcoal, pastel,
crayons, colored inks, and I have used photographs in
a collage. I have worked on paper, glass, wood, gesso
panels, canvas, and fabric. Of course I have to make
sure the medium will reproduce well. I have my
favorites, but when I reach out for something

different, I find that my approach to the old favorites is refreshed when I return to them.

You have to understand what each art director wants. You have to fulfill your obligation to the magazine, its special type of readers, and the author. And yet, with all this, there is so much opportunity to express yourself and develop something exciting. Sometimes people will ask me why I don't paint to please myself in my spare time. If I feel like experimenting in texture or abstract design I find a suitable time and place when I'm making an illustration.

Of course, much depends upon the author and the publication. You have all your gears set just so when you are working for one magazine. You know which colors they prefer and which type of composition they like for that particular publication. As you read the story, you can always tell what will make an illustration. In that sense you "see" the end result. When you're not familiar with the author, you have to read between the lines to get the mood. You should, of course, illustrate what's there. But when you are doing a story, you don't want to give the plot away. You don't want to tell everything, just enough to involve the reader and make him want to read. A "stopper" in an illustration will make the reader stop flipping pages and settle down to the story.

I've been asked to do a picture without being given any limitations and I find that it's difficult. It's like telling a comedian to "be funny." I always ask the art director something like, "Do you want a lot of red or yellow?"

Blue is a color that reproduces fairly accurately, so I tend to use it a lot if there is no reason not to. Once I've been given some point of departure with all the "musts" of page size, color, or whatever, I can take off from there.

I read the story over and over to get the mood. Sometimes I do a rough sketch or a color "comp" and submit it to the art director. Or we talk about the illustration over the telephone. I would rather do three illustrations a month instead of the eight or ten I used to do, so I can do justice to the assignment.

? *How do you get an art director to take a chance on something different?*

a In the first place, you give him something he did ask for as well as something new. You try to show him something that's better than anything he can think of.

Illustration. Oil. *McCall's*

If you spend a week thinking about it, it's bound to
be better. Sometimes an art director will give me a
rough that he's spent a couple of hours on. He knows
I'll spend a week on it and refine it.

Then, too, you have to remember that today an art
director generally wants something fresh—different.
It used to be that an art director would say, "Let's
call *him* because we know what we will get." Now he
says, "Let's get *him* and he'll give us something new—
different." The audiences are much more sophisticated
than they used to be.

? *Must you approach an illustration from the art
director's point of view as well as the artist's? For
example, you often lay out the whole page, complete
with type, white space and title.*

a I do like to make the layout for the page. I don't
want the illustration to look tacked onto the page.
Standing on the art director's side of the desk while
I work gives me the same satisfaction I get out of
playing with a bunch of jazz musicians. You are
totally involved. You become part of the thing.
I don't want to live the life of a hermit and create in
a corner.

170

**Al
Parker**

? *The "props" you use in your pictures are obviously
planned to be eyecatchers, but you never let them
detract from the composition of the whole illustration.
How do you manage to do it?*

a I don't use many props. The ones I do use are chosen
very carefully for their shape and form. They have to
help set the mood I am after. At the same time, they
have to have a certain timeless quality so that the
illustration will not look dated in a few months.
When the sack dress came in I was petrified that it
wouldn't last. After all, many months can go by
between the time you turn in the illustration and the
time the magazine comes out. I wanted to use the sack
but I was afraid it would be out of fashion. I ended
up using a dress that looked like the sack, but wasn't
that extreme. You have to be very aware of changing
tastes and be able to capture the mood of the moment,
what people are talking about and thinking about.

I can get as much inspiration out of an old poster
or a Victorian chair as I do out of the so-called
"important" subjects. There is a quality there or a
charm, and I react to it. Then I get all inspired.
I think this is a personal thing and depends upon the
individual. Anything belongs in a picture if it sparks
you. It all depends on how you look at things. A bar
of soap may no longer be a bar of soap when I look at
it, but a wonderful oval that surrounds the title of a
story. You should keep an open mind when you're an
illustrator. There's no reason to get stale. I think
there's so much to look at. Aside from technical
self-discipline, the most vital step toward
improvement is intelligent self-appraisal. You must
be honest with yourself.

As you read a manuscript, you should jot down
descriptions of the story background and its
characters. If you have a good research file, you can
quickly lay your hands on the important details
essential to an accurate rendering of scene and people.
I save pictures from magazines, bits of material,
photographs for my file. You never know what objects
you will be required to draw for an illustration. And
you shouldn't miss an opportunity to do something
authentic and exciting just because you couldn't get
hold of the right documentation at the right time.

I take pictures of places and people for my research
file whenever I go traveling. And when I am using a
model, the camera is a great help. I can work from
photographs when she is gone. The best thing is to use

Line drawing. Ink and pencil.
Courtesy of *Town and Country*.

live models all the time, but the fees are prohibitive.
For my illustrations I have to get high-fashion girls
and they come at a high price. The perfect way is to
draw from life because the color is before your eyes.

? *One of the illustrations you have used in this book as
an example of your work seems to be loaded with
props. I am referring to the picture of the little girl
pushing the carriage. Can you tell me where you
found such authentic detail?*

a This story carried very sinister overtones. The infant
in the pram is slated for death. I tried to give this
mood by choosing the neglected garden of the

orphanage for my setting. I was lucky to find an
actual pram of the period, complete with parasol.
I removed the latter, substituting for it flowers the
girl may have put there. This shows the girl's love for
the infant and also serves as a symbol. Having the
actual pram gave me a knowledge of the construction
of it and provided such added touches of realism as
the wooden wheel warped away from the metal
outer rim, the missing spoke and the unravelling
wicker parts on the body of the pram. I had other
research problems. The Brussels carpet used in those
days as a winter covering in the pram, was from a
clipping in my file. I found in the file a statue I liked.
I had photographed it in England, the locale of this
serial. The girl's costume was from a clipping.

When illustrating a costume story I always keep in
mind that this kind of story requires special care, if
the results are to be interesting. Dependence upon
costumes alone tends to make the story seem to be
just an old story dug up from the past and the
audience may feel it is too dry to read. Therefore,
I illustrate such stories in as fresh and human a
manner as possible. The characters in these stories
lived in the clothes they wore. They did not think of
them as costumes.

? *What was the most important thing you learned in art
school?*

a I learned to draw. It wasn't a knuckle-rapping school,
but at that time they frowned on modern and abstract
artists. They insisted on your being able to draw.
You can always depart from the academic in figures,
but you have to know how to draw well before you
can do it. I learned composition and color mostly by
doing. When I decided to become an illustrator,
I would cover up the illustrations in a new magazine
while I read the stories. Then I'd see what I could do.
I would make my own illustrations and compare them
with the original published pictures.

The craftsmanship comes in as you render. This is
something you must learn how to do and it is
indispensable. But the biggest part of the entire job
for me is creating the concept and composition. It all
has to flow and jell. This happens before you start
painting. This is the part that takes the longest time.

I have seen some oriental artists who had a natural
feeling for composition. But most of us must learn
to handle it, the way you have to learn to play scales
before you can play music.

17

NORMAN ROCKWELL

**22 famous
painters
and
illustrators
tell how
they work**

Photograph of the artist

Norman Rockwell is surely the best known and best loved American illustrator. He has been called "a pictorial Mark Twain" and his paintings have probably been seen and enjoyed by more people than those of any artist who ever lived. "I don't want to paint for the few who go to museums," he has said. "I want my pictures to be seen and enjoyed by people everywhere. I want them published." Born in New York City, Norman Rockwell spent his youth in the nearby suburban town of Mamaroneck. By the time he was fifteen, Rockwell had earned enough money doing odd jobs to be able to leave high school and go to art school. First, he attended the National Academy of Design. Later, he switched to the Art Students League where he studied with George Bridgman, the great authority on anatomy. He believes he learned the most important part of his craft from Bridgman. "I entered his class raw; I came out browned to a turn." Rockwell's first professional assignment was for a children's book. He was paid $150 for twelve drawings. This was the beginning of a long and lucrative career in art. Rockwell is perhaps best known for his *Saturday Evening Post* covers and illustrations. He has done hundreds of them. But he has also created countless advertising pictures and book and magazine illustrations.

My worst enemy is the earthshaking idea. I just can't handle it. It's beyond me, above me. I say what I want to say in terms of ordinary people in everyday situations. And I find I can fit almost anything into that framework, even fairly big ideas—like freedom of speech or freedom of worship. Fine pictures can come out of ordinary human experience.

? *The subjects you choose for your illustrations are nearly always country men and women. You don't seem interested in urban faces. Does this have to do with your early life or the fact that you live in a rural community now?*

a It is true that country people fit into my kind of picture better than city people. Their faces seem so open and expressive. But there are other reasons. If I lived in New York, I could never do anything. I was brought up in New York City, but I always wanted to be a country boy. I saw some awful things in New York. Up in the country I can have close relationships.

The Adventures of Huckleberry Finn. Oil.
With permission of The Heritage Press

I know everybody in town. I want more from people
than I can get in the city.

I don't know if I have a philosophy as an artist.
I do know that you must be extremely human to be
an artist. You have to take all the ills that flesh is
heir to, the sadness and joys, if you're going to be a
human-interest painter. I've had an awful lot of this.
I've lived in boardinghouses with alcoholics, failures,
the aunt that nobody could tolerate. I've traveled,
and I've seen a lot. You have to expose yourself to
life if you're going to be an artist—you have to
know the feel and smell of what you paint. You must
have curiosity. If you hear a scream you should go and

find out what's going on. It's your business, and it might make a good picture, or even a *Post* cover.

I have been criticized for not painting the seamy side of life—but it doesn't bother me. I once tried to paint a gangster with blood dripping from his mouth. I couldn't do it. I know I'm disliked by some because my attitude annoys them. The view of life I communicate in my pictures excludes the sordid and the ugly. I feel my work is popular for this reason. Ours is a frightening world, and people are reassured by simple human decency. I paint a happy world, but that's what I see.

Norman Rockwell

? *Your models are amateurs. Don't you have to direct them so they will give you the pose or expression you want?*

a Directing models is an art in itself and is somewhat akin to the motion picture director's job. First, you must discard all your own dignity and vanity and get into the act yourself in order to induce your model to lay aside his own dignity so he will feel and express the emotion which you want to convey.

This is not always easy, either for you or the model, and once in awhile you will find a model who looks the part but who just cannot lay aside his own individuality and act like someone else. He just can't break down and act. Then you must thank him for trying and look for someone else.

Before a model even attempts to pose for me, I tell him the story I want my pictures to say because I want him to understand what I am trying to do, what I am trying to convey. Then I get into the pose myself and show him how I think it should be done. This indicates that I am willing to make a fool of myself if necessary. The model usually loosens up about this time and begins to get into the spirit of the thing.

Next I suggest that he or she try the pose. Usually he doesn't get it the first thing because he probably is not a professional actor and he is still self-conscious. But we keep at it, and, if my model has a bit of the ham in him, he eventually loses all self-consciousness and begins to act the part with real feeling and enthusiasm. It is when he reaches this stage that I take pictures of him with my candid camera.

When I am working to stimulate a model I stop at nothing. I wisecrack to make him laugh if that's the expression I want, or I almost weep to make him feel sad if that is required, and I shout my lungs out to

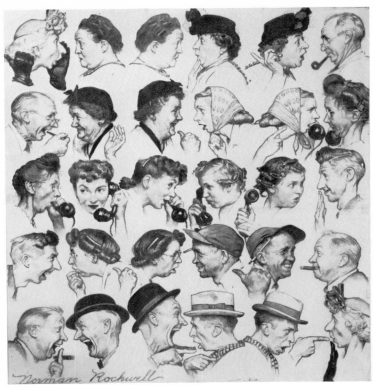

Gossip. Oil.
Reprinted by special permission of *The Saturday Evening Post.*
© 1948 The Curtis Publishing Company

excite him. Last but not least, I always pay a model
even if he is a bank president or one of my own
family.

? *Your gift for characterization has made you an
important artist. Yet, you have said that you are
more interested in storytelling than in portraiture.
Can you explain this a bit more?*

a I'm interested in why people behave as they do.
I don't like portraits. I want to tell a story, and
when I look at a person's face, I wonder what kind of
a story I can tell. I think you can make a great
painting out of any subject matter, but I think the
Renaissance painters who worked for the Church had
a terrific opportunity because they had wonderful

stories to tell. I know that when I did book illustrations I had a wonderful break when I was assigned a story by Stephen Vincent Benet.

Norman Rockwell

? *I have heard that you are a great admirer of Picasso and Matisse and that you carry color prints of these and other modern painters with you when you travel. Why, then, do you paint in such a representational manner when you clearly admire more experimental technique?*

a I simply couldn't do it. It wouldn't be natural for me. I have a great admiration for abstract art and modern painting. My oldest son is a modern painter. I'm all for experimentation in art. But my kind of storytelling isn't possible in abstract art.

I think Picasso is one of the greatest artists who ever lived, and certainly of our time, but I couldn't be Picasso. I love his work, except for his Blue Period, which he did because it was the popular thing to do. Actually, I agree with something Al Dorne said, that Picasso's tremendous influence as a force in painting and on artists in this century is more important than his personal art. I respect Matisse, Cézanne, and Klee, but my objection to modern art is the rigidity it demands. There seems to be so much emphasis on the misshapen, the broken down, the beaten.

Rembrandt has always been my favorite. Brueghel, Vermeer, and Ingres are draftsmen I admire. And in my student days, I was influenced by Joe Leyendecker and Howard Pyle. I think Howard Pyle made the greatest contribution to American illustration. And in more recent years, Al Parker. He has been most inventive. I do know that I could live quietly on a desert island with a few Howard Pyles and a single great Rembrandt.

? *You had a traditional art training at the Art Students League. If you had to start over again, would you seek the same kind of basic training?*

a Yes, although I'd probably finish high school before going to art school. I am very glad I learned to draw under such a teacher as George Bridgman. You have to know the rules before you can break them. Picasso, for example, is a very fine draftsman. A young illustrator should first of all learn to draw. He needs to learn how to use color and light and line.

People are always asking me what advice I would

Cover illustration. Oil.
Reprinted by special permission of *The Saturday Evening Post.*
© 1954 The Curtis Publishing Company

give a young illustrator or a student who wants to paint magazine covers. The first thing he must do is convince an art director that he can be trusted to do an acceptable job. And deliver it on time! If he has any published work to show, the art director may try him out. If he comes through, he'll get other jobs.

Then they ask me, "What about talent? Must you have unusual talent to be a successful artist?" It helps. Genius helps even more.

? *Would you describe your own methods of working? Which comes first, the emotional response to an idea, or an intellectual appraisal of its potential? Is picture making an exhilarating experience, or is it the sober application of craft to a problem?*

a I am always emotionally excited about an idea. But then I have to figure out how to execute the idea.

I don't actually see the end result of a painting
immediately. I may have an image of how it should
look, but as I work on it many things change. And the
picture may end up quite differently. Of course,
I have feelings about my work. I am happy when it's
going well and depressed quite often when I am sure
it will never come off. But I am chiefly absorbed in
making the picture work. My craft helps me to do this.

I think that illustration was cruder before artists
began to use cameras. But artists should leave
realism to the camera—which does many things
magnificently—and create something from their
imagination. I'll take maybe fifty photographs of
models of a scene I like. Then I'll pick the hands
from one and the nose from another, to use as guides
in painting. But they are only guides. The picture
I make comes out of me. I'm not an illustrator any
more. I do genre.

When I started out as an illustrator, I worked
chiefly for children's magazines. That's why I'm so
fond of painting kids and dogs. My style did develop
over the years as I noticed other artists and the way
they worked. But as I said before, I got my basic
training as a draftsman from George Bridgman at the
Art Students League. You start out by following other
artists like a spaniel. Then, if you've got it in
you, you become yourself—a lion.

? *One of the most remarkable qualities in any Rockwell
painting is its humor. You convey a warm
appreciation of the frailties of human nature without
depending upon cruelty or bitterness for your effect.
How do you accomplish this difficult feat?*

a I think humor has to have some pain with it. I once
did a cover showing a father seeing his son off to
college. That year my three boys had gone away and
I'd had an empty feeling—it took me a while to
adjust without them. This poignancy was what I
wanted to get across in the picture. But there was
humor in it, too. I put a funny kind of suit on the boy
because he was a ranch boy leaving home for the first
time. And his father was holding two hats, one the
boy's beat-up old rancher's hat and the other his
brand-new hat. The boy was carrying a lunch box all
done up in a pink ribbon. I drew a collie dog with
his head on the boy's lap. My son said, "You can't
put that dog in. That's too much." But I was right.
You see the father couldn't show how he felt about
the boy's leaving. The dog did.

Freedom of Worship. Oil.
Reprinted by special permission of *The Saturday Evening Post.*
© 1943 The Curtis Publishing Company

? *Every artist has trouble getting ideas. How do you keep your apparently bottomless idea file of situations and people brimful?*

a I like to do my idea-thinking in one long session. I get six or eight ideas for covers okayed by the *Post* at one time. That takes care of me for six months, what with advertising assignments and other jobs. Then when I get down to doing my fifth *Post* cover of the batch, I know it's time to think of some new ideas. I keep a file of possible ones, letters from readers, clippings, and notes. Of course, I have a lot of ideas and impressions in my head. And I think of

people I know and would like to paint. There must
be some way to use Tom Kerry, I'll say to myself.
What would Tom Kerry be likely to do? I have a
terrible time with ideas. The first day I go at it I'm
convinced that I'm through, that I'll never get
another idea in my life. But the next day things look
up. The problem is to finish off an idea with a twist.
I am lucky because I have a good memory. I do
remember a lot. I did a cover not long ago based on
something I saw in England twenty years ago. I had
an idea for a cover based on gossips that I played with
for thirty years before I could figure out how to finish
it off with the right twist. I thought everybody would
be mad if I showed them gossiping as though I was
critical of what they did. Then I had an idea. I simply
put myself in the picture as one of the gossips.

? *Do you think up your own ideas?*

a I have to do it this way. It has to be all me. My
baby. And in this first stage I think this idea of
mine is really the most beautiful. I'm all excited.
My enthusiasm for an idea lasts until the second stage
of making a picture. This is when I begin to sag a
little when I am applying craft. I have to discipline
myself to finish it. Then, when it emerges as a
tangible thing, it comes as a relief.

? *One of the things that becomes immediately apparent
about your work is that you thoroughly enjoy
painting. Could you tell me why?*

a I paint to fulfill myself. I paint the kind of world
I think should exist. And then, too, I paint to make
money and please people. There's nothing so relaxing
as painting except when there's a due date and the
kids need food. I love it. I think there's an awful
lot of hidden talent around. People can have fun with
art even if they don't make a profession of it.
   Getting paid is nice for a lot of reasons. I've
always been paid. But sometimes I wonder what a
painting is worth. I once got paid an amount equal to
the price of three Ford cars. When you put a painting
up next to three big cars—it really makes you think!
   I am happy when I do something well. But I love
the letters I get. I'm just a ham actor. Of course, I'd
love to have the critics notice me, too. I never worry
about being typecast. It's too late now. It's wonderful
when you don't have to worry any longer.

18

BEN SHAHN

**22 famous
painters
and
illustrators
tell how
they work**

Photograph of the artist

Ben Shahn's reputation as one of the truly original painters of our time is based on both his commercial and fine arts work. He approaches every assignment he accepts with enthusiasm and integrity, and his paintings reflect a compassion for the human condition. Leo Lionni, Art Director of *Fortune*, has effectively described the impact of "a Shahn" on the public eye: "from drawings so lean and penetrating one would expect bitterness, but the compassion for man's loneliness, the sympathy for man's misery, the joy for man's little pleasures are always present. It is little wonder that . . . a Shahn drawing or painting erupts with an irresistible urgency which awakens spent eyes and calloused hearts." Born in Kaunas, Russia, Ben Shahn came to America in 1906. He worked as a lithographer's apprentice during the day and attended high school at night. Later he studied at New York University and the City College of New York. Leaving City College in 1922, he attended the National Academy of Design. Ben Shahn had his first one-man exhibition at the Downtown Gallery, in New York City, in 1930. He worked on the Rockefeller Center frescoes in 1932-33 with Diego Rivera. A decade later, he did the murals in fresco for the Social Security Building in New York City. Shahn's work hangs in public collections at the University of Michigan; the Baltimore Museum of Art; the Fogg Art Museum in Cambridge, Massachusetts; Dartmouth College; Wadsworth Atheneum; the Metropolitan Museum of Art; the Museum of Modern Art; Smith College Museum; The Phillips Gallery, and others. He lives with his wife, artist Bernarda Bryson, in Roosevelt, New Jersey.

Content

If you're going to be an artist, all life is your subject. And all your experience is part of your art. A youngster told me recently that he was going to give himself a year to see if he had talent. A year! It takes a lifetime to see if you have it. Painting is a total engagement.

? *You don't believe in ivory towers, then?*

a No, I don't approve of those beautiful isolated artists' communities apart from the world.
You should paint what is around you—things, people, landscapes you are familiar with.

185

Blind Botanist. Tempera.
Wichita Art Museum, Roland P. Murdock Collection

? *What do you try to communicate?*

a My own feelings about life. These feelings can be
expressed in a still life or a picture of the bomb.
I feel that many of the tools of art—colors, textures,
shapes—have become ends in themselves. I want to
communicate more than the tools. My father was a
cabinetmaker, and he was concerned with keeping his
tools in good order. But the important thing was to
use the tools. A work of art must communicate a kind

of philosophy, make me laugh or cry. I've been dubbed a "social" painter. I feel that anyone who puts brush to paper is a social painter. Every fear and hope and desire of mankind is my particular interest. In "The Blind Botanist," for example, I am trying to show man's progress through life. A blind man *would* be a botanist. In "The Red Stairway" the crippled man is climbing upward. I wanted to say something about the indestructibility of mankind.

Ben Shahn

? *Why do you draw or paint as you do? How did your style evolve?*

a Style will naturally follow you if you learn to be yourself. You cannot separate style from the content or the meaning of the picture. People who talk ceaselessly about style are talking about a gimmick. When I draw, I use a brush instead of a pen because I was a lithographer, and we used to draw on stone with a brush. I can draw as fine a line with a brush as with a pen. This is no affectation. It is part of my early training and an inseparable part of myself.

? *How do you go about making a picture, and how analytical are you in doing it?*

a I begin with an idea. I say to myself, this is going to be a picture *about* such and such. Then, when I begin to do it, it may not resemble the first image. In the middle of a painting I often clarify my work with drawings. I have described the relationship between the painter and his painting as a conversation back and forth, the painting telling the painter even as it receives its shape and form. From the moment the painter begins to strike figures of color upon a surface, he must become acutely sensitive to the feel, the textures, the light, the relationships that arise before him. At one point he will mold the material according to an intention. At another he may yield the intention—perhaps his whole concept—to emerging forms, to new implications within the painted surface. Thus the idea rises to the surface, grows, changes as a painting grows and develops.

? *Do you think painters tend to develop the same ideas over and over again?*

a Yes, there is the recurrent image. When you hear the name Van Gogh, you get an image. Most painters convey a certain image or way of thinking.

Red Stairway. Tempera.
Collection of City Art Museum of St. Louis

? *What would you say yours is?*

a This is going to be hard. It's about people—men, women—I am always so concerned with this business of tension and conflict.

? *The tension of life is always conveyed in your pictures, but it is not uncomfortable for the viewer. You communicate a kind of nonanxious anxiety. It makes me want to know what is happening in the picture, what went before and what will come later. Are you recreating something that you have experienced emotionally or intellectually?*

a This is a very dangerous area. How do any of us experience anything? Through our eyes and ears, certainly. I only know that I feel strongly about the things I paint or I wouldn't care to paint them.

? *Then you feel the choice of subject matter is up to the painter? If he wants to paint the family-automobile instead of a red barn, that's perfectly all right?*

a There is not a thing in the world that won't make a worthwhile subject. No one thing is more moving than another. Whatever crosses the human mind may be fit content for art—in the right hands. Of course, you may find a wonderful subject but lack the technical equipment to do what you want to do. A critic once wrote that an apple by Cézanne was better than a Madonna by Raphael. And I thought at the time that a Madonna by Cézanne would have been better than an apple by Raphael. Don't look for something pretty, but for something that has meaning. The pair of shoes that Van Gogh painted has an importance that a lot of other paintings of infinitely worthy subjects do not. You don't have to switch subjects if you continue to be interested in one and it challenges you. A painter named Morandi does nothing but bottles. For forty-five years he has been painting bottles. The important thing is to choose a subject that you either hate or love. Never paint something you have no strong feelings about.

? *Having chosen a subject, how should the student painter begin to work?*

a He must look at it as if he has never seen it before. If he can see it through his own eyes and through nobody else's he will have something unique. The general tendency of students is to go off in a direction that is currently popular—the one that is attracting the favorable adjectives. He should resist this temptation. The function of the artist is to show his feelings about the outer world, or his own inner world, through *his* eyes.

? *Is it loss of nerve that makes so many students imitate the best sellers?*

a It might be. We all need protection. Every one of us wants approval and if we see that a certain direction of art is greatly approved we think we'll do that and we'll get approval. But it doesn't work that way. When I see a man trying to paint like Gauguin and that man has never been to the South Seas or had any of Gauguin's inner experiences, I know it won't work. The hardest thing to get across to a student is that he must find out who he is, what his talents are.

? *This takes a lot of courage, doesn't it, to stick to your convictions? To be a nonconformist?*

a Oh, yes, it takes courage. I don't care what the conviction is—you must be fearless and follow it.

Silent Music. Brush drawing. CBS

Nonconformity to me means quite simply a want of satisfaction with things as they are. The creative person—the nonconformist—may be in profound disagreement with the present way of things, or he may simply wish to express his views, to render a personal account of matters.

? *I think one of the most interesting things about your career is that you have been successful in both fine and commercial art. I know you believe the two are compatible. Could you explain why?*

a I am always shocked at the notion that there are two separate worlds, commercial art and fine art. The commercial artist who should be happy with his craft too often feels discontented. Talent per se may exist to a greater degree in a commercial artist than in a fine artist. How the talent is used depends on the brain that goes with it, of course. About a tenth of my work is commercial, and I enjoy it.

? *And you don't shift gears, so to speak, when you turn from painting a picture to making an advertisement?*

a When I am called upon to do something, I do the best I know how and treat it with the same respect I give

anything else. Then I become stubborn about any
changes. There are artists who curse the art director
when he says, "Very nice, but . . ." and suggests
changes. They may curse him privately, but publicly
they ask, "When do you want it?"

? *Can you give me an example of your stubbornness
about making changes in your completed work?*

a I once made a drawing called "Silent Music" for a
broadcasting company. When I brought it in, the art
director showed a great deal of enthusiasm for the
work. Everyone else was well pleased, too. Then they
noticed there was no microphone in the picture. Just
empty chairs and music stands. They asked me if
I could put the mike somewhere in the drawing.
I worked at it but I honestly couldn't find a place for
the mike. I told them that the picture had been
planned without it and it would be impossible to
insert it now. But I suggested that I draw a little
mike which could be dropped in the copy and which
would identify the broadcaster. This solution made
everybody happy.

? *Many of the illustrations you have done for magazines
or advertising agencies now hang in private
collections. They seem to have a life of their own
apart from the "selling" job they did originally.*

a One of the magazine art directors used to say of me,
"Ben doesn't care if he's paid or if his work is
published. He just wants the original back." When
I started insisting on this, other artists did so, too.
The picture belongs to the artist. I'm as proud of
these pictures as of anything I've done.

? *Do you create these ads or illustrations to suit an
image the art director has of the end result?
I would imagine that few art directors would leave the
concept entirely in your hands.*

a Once an agency asked me to do an ad and they sent
me a rough sketch of what they wanted. They had
imitated my style and sketched in a "Shahn-type"
drawing. I sent it back with a note refusing the
commission. They had taken all the fun out of it.
I told them I did not want to reproduce someone
else's idea. The only joy left is the joy of discovery.

Sunday Painting. Water color and gouache.
Collection of Mrs. Ben Shahn.
Courtesy of Downtown Gallery

? *Do you think it's easier for you to be stubborn when faced with the constrictions of commercial art because of your reputation? They are, after all, getting a name and an individual style. If they seek you out, they should be prepared for an individual piece of work.*

a I was exactly forty-four years old before someone asked me to do a commercial piece of work. My aesthetic arteries had hardened by then. One art director told me that he would never use my work if he really had to sell something, because I couldn't glamorize a product and make it more than it is. I asked him why he used me at all and he said my work attracted more attention than that of the others he'd used.

? *I've heard that your work is in such demand that your paintings are sold before they are even finished.*

a That's a romantic notion. There are people who hope I'll paint something that they want, and I'm glad to say that my work does sell very well. Some years ago,

192

after an exhibition of my paintings opened, my wife said, "Don't you think *we* can afford one now?"

? *An art critic once said that your work is more representational than most abstraction, but it still carries a complex message. How do you feel about abstract art?*

Ben Shahn

a The word abstraction has been so abused it has lost all meaning. To abstract is to draw out the essence of a matter. But you must abstract from something. Facility without content means nothing.

? *What do you look for in a picture?*

a I always identify myself first with the patterning, the shapes of things. Then I go closer, and I am probably affected most by color and the last thing is content. I work in just the opposite way. But to the person looking at a picture, I think the most obvious thing is pattern.

? *What artists, now working, would you like to collect?*

a No artist in his entirety. It's the individual picture that moves me.

? *Which artists influenced you most in your period of development?*

a The Florentines and the Siennese, mostly because of their precision. When I went to Europe, the Impressionists were important. But when I saw Florentine art, I realized that this was much closer to what I wanted to do.

? *What use is a picture anyway?*

a What use is there in living? I don't really know. You can't eat or smell a picture. But it's something that can move you. I feel that each work of art—each serious work—has an intrinsic value. It was made to contain permanently something that was felt and thought and believed. It contains that feeling, and nothing else.

For me a picture must have some broad philosophy of the painter which comes through. Then it must have the tools. These are important. What if you had the loftiest idea but didn't know how to communicate it to others?

Ben Shahn

? *What should a beginning painter know about the craft of making pictures once he has determined the direction he will take?*

a He must know the tools of his craft because, like the cabinetmaker, he is interested in creating something that will last. Making a table for a cafeteria or for royalty employs the same craftsmanship.

? *How important is drawing to the total result of a picture?*

a To me it's terribly important. In commercial art you simply have to be able to draw.

? *Many students ask why you distort certain elements in your pictures when you know how to draw them in scale or perspective. Your hands, for example, are always prominent and rather primitive looking. Why?*

a I do this deliberately because that's the way I feel about them. It is even more important to put down what you feel than what you see.

? *And yet you believe strongly in documentation? And realism?*

a Yes. There is a difference in the way a twelve-dollar coat wrinkles and the way a seventy-five-dollar coat wrinkles, and that has to be right. It's just as important aesthetically as the difference in the light of the city of Paris and the Brittany Coast. Maybe it's more important. But it's also important to have a play back and forth between the big and the little, the light and the dark, the smiling and the sad, the serious and the comic.

? *Tell me, how much time do you spend in your studio each day?*

a I'm out there right after breakfast and I work until my wife calls me to lunch. I go back there again until about six in the evening.

? *Even on weekends?*

a Even then, except when I realize I have been working steadily for several weeks, so I grit my teeth and relax.

? *I know you studied abroad for quite some years as a young man. What other formal art education did you* *have—and if you had it to do over again, would you choose a different kind of training?*

a I went to the National Academy of Design, which is a good trade school. I lived in Europe for about four years and went to school most of the time when I was there, working from models and plaster casts. I did go through a devil of a lot of that. From the time I was fifteen until I was thirty I went to one school or another, whether it was a sketch class or one with a live model. And I wouldn't do any differently today. One of the youngsters who lives near me was horrified to hear that I had gone to school so long. She wants to be an artist but she doesn't want to study art. I asked her what she liked doing best and she said jitterbugging, and she did it two or three nights a week. I told her, "I was luckier than you. I could do the thing I loved every night of the week when I went to art school." In Paris I went to the Academy for about three years. I was trained as a lithographer, you see, so I could earn quite a bit of money when I needed it and then go away for a stretch of time and study art. I recently gave my daughter, who is an artist, and her husband some of the prize money I had won to help them afford a trip abroad. It is important to look at art and study it. I told them I was giving them "a fathership" so they could go.

? *Must a successful artist have talent?*

a Talent is an ingredient, certainly. But I've seen talented people burn out if there's nothing upstairs. Originality, to me, is when a person is totally himself. And so, developing originality is not something one does in a purposeful way, it is simply the outgrowth of a person. It's an organic change.

? *Summing it up, what advice would you give the student painter or illustrator?*

a I would have him go through a very rigorous training. If he has any reservations about his courses or his teachers, he should listen, but keep it to himself. If he looks at all illustrators working today he can find out what he wants to avoid as well as what he admires. He should know all that he can about art and by all means have opinions. He should try hard to learn to draw or paint better than he already does, and never be afraid to undertake any kind of art at all, however exalted or however common. The important thing is to try to do it with distinction.

19

SYD SOLOMON

**22 famous
painters
and
illustrators
tell how
they work**

Photograph of the artist

Chosen in 1954 as one of "27 Americans with a
Future" by *Art in America* magazine, Syd Solomon has
justified his early promise. His paintings hang in the
Wadsworth Atheneum, the Baltimore Museum of Art,
the Whitney Museum, the Birmingham Museum, and
the Walter Chrysler Museum, among others. Solomon
has received the Gold Medal of Honor, Audubon
Artists, 1957; the Florida International Purchase
Award, 1952; the First Award, Society of Painters in
Casein, Riverside Museum, 1957; and the First
Purchase Award, National Oil, Sarasota Art
Association, 1958. Born in Uniontown, Pennsylvania,
Solomon studied art briefly at the Chicago Art
Institute and L'Ecole des Beaux Arts in Paris. During
World War II Solomon served as camouflage engineer
and reconnaissance artist in five battle campaigns as
well as the Normandy landings. Determinedly
experimental, Solomon regards himself as a self-taught
artist. He has learned to paint through experience.
The results are daring and, to some, even startling.
As one Solomon collector put it, "I do not 'look' at
such paintings. They confront me." The artist lives
with his wife and two children in Sarasota, Florida,
during the winter. In the summer the Solomons move
north to another spot favored by painters, East
Hampton, New York.

**Media
and
Techniques**

In the beginning, I had no real understanding of art.
I was just interested in skillful virtuosity. I don't
think I knew a good painting from a bad one. I still
think art education has to be faced. The artist should
learn existing aesthetics and art history. Many of
those who might have something to say as artists never
do discover their real abilities because they don't
know enough about art. While it's fine to use tools
and reproduce what you see, you must also know what
great art of the past is about to form your own ideas
with some maturity.

? *The new art materials have had a tremendous impact
on the art world, haven't they?*

a Recently I have had an accelerated awareness of
just what this impact can mean to the total art world,
largely because a group of researchers and writers are
racing to bring out the first comprehensive reports on
these new techniques. They now want to make a
record of the beginnings of a new decade of plastics,

Pendent. Oil-tempera. Collection of Albert Dorne

polymers and other new adhesives in the use of art.
I have been listed by them as one of the first (in 1952)
to employ some of these mixtures in easel painting.
I am pleased if some of my involvement has given to
others a greater technical opportunity. I have no
training in the laboratory. All of the scientific work
in developing the extraordinary range of new
materials has been done by others. I always have been
concerned about the permanence of materials and
have tried to understand their limitations.
I now see many reckless mixtures of supports,
grounds, paint film and varnishes in this technical
revolution. Some of the new adhesives have proved

to be dangerously toxic when used without proper precautions. Other casual uses have produced flaking in the painting and fugitive effects. I hope that the surge of experimentation will continue but with greater study in the scientific area. We need expert advice from laboratory technicians before we can adopt the new materials on an unqualified basis.

Syd Solomon

? *You have become widely known as an innovator in experimentation with new painting materials. How did you earn that reputation?*

a If I am known as an innovator—it is largely because of the urgings of a research chemist who kept delivering what he called "Twentieth-century adhesives" to my studio. I tried them all. Some of them seemed to have advantages over traditional mediums. Perhaps due to his persistence, I used some of them for the first time in the development of easel painting. Then I was asked to write papers about these new plastics and resins and mixtures. These new techniques offer what I believe is an expanded vocabulary for the student, but he must always realize in adopting them that technique in itself, if it shows, can be tricky and is rarely convincing—it is no substitute for content. And even so, the newness is often in drying acceleration and similar work-in-progress processes that don't necessarily show in the final work.

? *But you are still doing a great job of experimenting with contemporary painting materials?*

a Yes, Most artists experiment. Perhaps because we must invent to go on. We are always making a new form, a new color, a new spatial arrangement. Why not a new medium?

If you can make your work sufficiently original, it just doesn't matter what your subject is or what kind of glue holds it together, whether it is linseed oil or acrylic plastic. The few minutes of excitement you might enjoy when you think you have created something new are always followed by the sobering, sometimes depressing thought that someone may ask you to describe that moment of discovery that made you strike out and alter something in your method of working. Was it the application of logic? Was it pure feeling? Was it made with some new medium discovery? All tough questions—who really knows the answers?

Signal. Oil-tempera. Brandeis University Collection, gift of Dr. and Mrs. Rudolph Drosd

Yes, I continue to experiment, but I know that the image I have must fit the material since the material will be the image.

? *You believe, then, that originality is most important?*

a I think it is important, but there is something even more important. The artist must be aware. He should understand the purpose and meaning of art, or else how can he determine originality? Just being yourself has no meaning unless you first know what others have done.

It seems reasonable to me that the proper painting habits can be taught and are being taught, but the preparation of the student for a personal direction can rarely be taught. It must be sought for by the student himself.

One of the greatest difficulties with the student painter is frequently his inability, through lack of funds or interest, to see a lot of art. A student should get excited enough by the prospect of being a painter to want to look at great art. I believe that this looking at enough art is the one thing that the school and the teacher cannot provide. The student must do it for himself. If someone is an excellent student, if he does interesting work and is praised by the teacher, he often thinks he is all set. But he must do more. The first thing he can do is to delve into art history.

**Syd
Solomon**

I say all of this because I feel that my own way of going would have been expedited by greater understanding and knowledge of painting. I had to learn this for myself after I had made mistakes in direction. I perhaps could have eliminated my mistakes if I had had greater awareness. I've always been very eager to give away as soon as possible any technical discoveries. I have never been tempted to substitute technique for art. I never emphasized techniques as a mystery. They were all either used by me or taught by me for reasons of unusual qualities that they alone could provide, or simply to save time. I wanted to provide the student with an accelerated entry into the problems of artistic decision-making. I wanted to go beyond the usual slow method of teaching.

Frequently, it is better to initiate the student as swiftly as possible in the problems of painting, and then if the student produces some interesting accidents, he will know how necessary it is for him to improve in other ways. Then he will be motivated to master such disciplines as color and composition.

? *What made you want to become an artist if, as you say, you had no awareness of the meaning of art?*

a As long as I can remember I have been painting. In grade school I was the guy who volunteered to do the painting and drawing and that art stuff. I had teachers who were interested in me in high school and helped me. I was a good athlete, too, so I had to make a decision between an art scholarship and athletic scholarship. I ended up taking neither. The colleges that wanted me to play football had no fine arts instruction. The colleges that gave me an art

The Silent World. Oil-tempera. Ringling Museum of Art

scholarship wanted me to make posters. That is changed today.

Instead I took irregular courses at the Chicago Art Institute. I had all kinds of jobs. I moved around the country a great deal. I always kept some kind of painting going. I sketched. I always felt if I had to earn a living it was better to do something connected with art. I did advertising art, newspaper art, and posters. I could draw well and had sort of a flair for layout.

When World War II started, I was called in by Homer St. Gaudens to join other artists in forming the first camouflage battalion. We had tough combat engineer training, but continued to use our art experience. I did many original camouflage designs. It was all challenging and interesting, but ceased after

D day when we quickly reverted to our more useful combat training.

After the war, I studied in Paris and then came to Sarasota, Florida, which has a fabulous coastline on the Gulf of Mexico. I painted and I fished, and became interested in the landscape beneath the sea as well as above.

Syd Solomon

? *What is it about the water that stimulates you as an artist?*

a I am fascinated by the sea. Maybe it's because I was born so far from it, in the mountains of Pennsylvania in a coal-mining town. I became interested in the world beneath the sea.

I even had a diving bell so I could go down and look at the sea from below. I like the reefs near Bimini. I like the push and pull of the currents, also the up and down currents. The sea is the last free place left in the world.

I am rather awed and inspired by it. It's where I'm able to fashion my personal myth. I'm interested in the ebb and flow of tidal waters, and what happens to the land and the rocks battered by the tidal flow for millions of years. I like the birds that work in or near the sea more than other birds. The idea of birds is also in much of my work. I've tended in the last year or two to take a greater step toward vertical movement. It started with my thoughts about the origin of flying and birds. All of this has led me to an appreciation of Poussin and the way he and Raphael could arrest vertical motion.

? *Would you say that you get most of your painting ideas then from nature?*

a It has not been my choosing a subject but the subject choosing me. Something must motivate it. In my case it's love. I'm sure there are other forces operating in any choice of ideas.

? *Do you plan a picture quite deliberately, making many sketches before you actually set out to do the final painting?*

a There is no need for me to make sketches of ideas that have been so close to me for so long. Some people make diagrammatic drawings, and that's fine with me. But I prefer to keep to the big idea and perfect it and let it grow as I'm working. My way of producing a

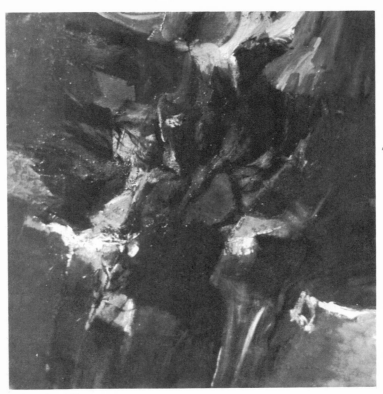

Take Rise. Oil-tempera.
Collection of the Whitney Museum of American Art, New York.
Anonymous gift

picture is so private that if I tried to describe it, I'd only be making up something because I didn't want to reveal the truth, or just didn't have the means to reveal the truth.

I would always champion a great amount of drawing for any painter. To my knowledge no painter of any consequence has come forward—no matter what his final idea is so far as subject or nonsubject is concerned—unless he has had some academic training—and that means drawing. A lot of it.

? *How much intellect do you think goes into painting?*

a Frequently in fiction and mass-media articles, the painter has been depicted as a rough character who hasn't followed the intellectual poses of other creative professionals. The moviemakers and playwrights have often presented the painter as a romantic Bohemian, usually starving, usually desperate, and always different-looking. But on learning more about many legendary artists' lives, on reading their published papers, we realize how many of them have been men of rare intelligence and erudition. Today, because of more desire on the part of the public to hear the artist speak out—in interviews like this one and in other ways, the point of view toward artists has changed.

**Syd
Solomon**

? *What do you think about the direction modern art has taken in the last few years?*

a The direction of art in the last few years has seemed almost a calculated maneuver to shake my spirit from day to day. It has brought me awareness of the desperation of the artist to symbolize the desire to give form to life. It has been a great period. It has been a dark devouring period. At its most lucid, a spiritual rebirth. At its most difficult, a trifle of frustration and fashion. It has been a challenging time to be painting.

I have looked particularly for (and found frequently) the inspired, whether in the great, crucial, recurrent themes of nature or the revelations of increased abstraction. The last ten years have given us a paradox of denials and affirmations. Art in America has appeared that is aware of the rest of the world, yet does not imitate it. I am proud of being part of this, yet I cannot ever go along with the transcontinental rivalry which seems more geographic than artistic.

? *What artists have influenced your work?*

a I honor many masters. The list changes from year to year. Through the years, I have become less and less interested in sentimentality and narrative qualities—frequently remembering the visual impact of a great painting long after I have forgotten who or what it was supposed to be about.

I invariably look for the painting to provide me with an insight to the man—Picasso has certainly done this for me. The artist must absolutely nakedly reveal himself.

I have no other message than to seduce the eye of the observer, and to make something beautiful in a way it has never been made before.

20

BEN STAHL

**22 famous
painters
and
illustrators
tell how
they work**

Photograph of the artist

Ben Stahl believes that illustration can benefit immeasurably from a fine arts approach. He has succeeded in proving his point over a long career as a top illustrator. His editorial and advertising pictures have the richness and texture of fine paintings. Born in Chicago, Stahl was encouraged to be an artist by his grandmother. She took him to visit the Chicago Art Institute and other galleries. She bought paints and brushes for him to use, and urged him toward a career in art. When Stahl was in the seventh grade he was named the most promising art student in his school and awarded a scholarship to the Chicago Art Institute. In 1927 he got a job as an apprentice in a Chicago art studio and began to apply himself to commercial work. As he acquired a knowledge of his craft, he was given more responsibility for creating illustrations. Five years later he showed his portfolio of samples to the head of a top art studio in Chicago, and was hired as an illustrator to work on their leading advertising and editorial accounts. Stahl worked in studios in Chicago and Detroit, spent some years as an illustrator for the Chicago *Daily News*. A marine painting he did for an advertisement caught the eye of the *Saturday Evening Post,* and Stahl began getting magazine assignments. In 1943 he moved to New York to be near art markets there. Then, in 1953, he and his wife built a home in Sarasota, Florida, where they live during the few months of the year when Stahl is not traveling around the world on art assignments.

Romanticism

Pure art is timeless. Degas once said, "The air in a great painting is unbreathable." A great painting makes people work to understand it. I maintain that painting is static in the best sense of the word. It's not supposed to do anything for anybody except just be there, just exist. It dominates the room it is in, the people, everything.

? *You have successfully translated the spirit of fine art into illustration. Although you are thought of as a romantic painter, your illustrations for editorial and advertising media have a strong selling power. Could you comment on the way in which you worked out a synthesis of fine art and commercial art?*

a In illustration we are concerned with what goes on, with what is happening in a literary way. In other

White Church. Oil. Courtesy of John Hancock Mutual Life Insurance Company

words, we are concerned with "story." In pure art, story is renounced. The important thing is the emotional impact that the abstract structure of the forms has on the viewer. The artist doesn't give a hoot for the story or the subject matter, but is only concerned with the underlying mood. The subject is merely a vehicle the artist uses to express emotion through the abstract structure.

Illustration *can* be great art, but only when the artist refuses to imitate slavishly what the writer says and instead says in a *new* way the guts of what the writer had in mind. And most important of all, the illustrator must not illustrate in too literary a manner. Literature is the author's domain, not the painter's. Rembrandt did a lot of illustration; take a close look at his work and you will see what I mean.

? *Do you think there is antagonism toward modern art today?*

a There has always been throughout history antagonism toward "modern art," because it represented change. If we had no change in art it would mean that art was denying a basic law of nature which is, simply, a need for change.

? *What qualities do you look for in a picture, and what kind of enjoyment do you expect to get?*

Ben Stahl

a I don't actually *look* for anything in a picture except to find out how it was done. If it is great it gives me something without any effort on my part. I don't get what you would call enjoyment. The word enjoyment is totally inadequate. A feeling of helpless weakness, accompanied by gooseflesh and utter amazement, is what I feel when standing before a truly great work of art. This is followed by the thought (and then the act of getting my nose as close to it as possible), How in the world did he do it? Next I wonder what I can learn from this thing so that my own work will be better. *A great painting is the greatest art instructor in the world!* If only you allow it to speak to you. All the secrets and mysteries are there, exposed for all to see and learn. This is why students should buy the work of their betters. Reproductions are fine, but only in the original can you find *all* the answers.

? *What makes a good picture?*

a The same mysterious something that makes Life.

? *Your illustrations have the texture and richness of fine art. Can you give us some examples of the painting techniques you use to achieve this effect?*

a I do not lay out a palette methodically before beginning to paint, but squeeze out a few colors at first and then add others to the palette from time to time as I find I need them. Sometimes I progress from four or five colors to as many as fifteen or sixteen, though I consider it wise to limit the palette, generally speaking. The use of too much color, particularly at the beginning, tends to confuse.

One should not try for the ultimate color effect of the picture at the start. In the early stages of the painting the important thing is to state the general shapes and forms, and establish the large pattern. Begin by using umbers, Mars yellow, white and black, with perhaps a little cerulean or cobalt blue. The variety of color one can get from such a limited palette is amazing. After the major forms have been established, you can add more and more color to the

Jack of Swords. Casein.
Reprinted by special permission of *The Saturday Evening Post.*
© 1949 The Curtis Publishing Company

picture where it is needed—and only where it is needed.

The method I have described is basically that developed and used by the old masters. I have adapted it to my way of working and added a number of ideas borrowed from the methods of the Impressionists. This approach is by no means the only way to handle color. It is simply my usual procedure, which I vary as the occasion requires.

I use an old formula for underpainting. I mix equal parts of French chalk powder and zinc white powder and add enough Valspar to give it a slight golden tinge. This formula lasts like iron on the canvas and will never crack or peel off. It also gives a luminous quality to the painting.

? *Do you use a camera in your work?*

a Sure. But it hasn't influenced my work in the slightest. I make the photograph my slave, I am not a slave to it.

? *Who, in your opinion, made the greatest contribution to American illustration?*

a Howard Pyle. But the photograph buried handmade illustrations. I believe, though, that it was a premature burial. (The corpse seems these days to be kicking a little.) It's up to the young illustrator of today to dig him up.

? *What artists influenced you most in your development?*

Ben Stahl

a First it was Paul Bransom. Then Frank Hoffman, followed by Roy Spreter. Mostly, though, in later years, it was Degas and Renoir. El Greco excites me most these days. Although I am not as impressionable as I used to be, I would like to collect any artist, whatever his name, whose work involves me.

? *What, to your way of thinking, is the best kind of art training?*

a I had no art-school training. I left one wasted year of high school behind to take a job running errands for a commercial art studio. I did do a tremendous amount of drawing and taught myself the fundamentals of art.

Becoming an artist is a full-time job. To arrive at the goal you must proceed in a straight line, slowly, thoughtfully, holding your principles high. You should put emphasis on one subject at a time and study it thoroughly. Concentrate on anatomy for six or eight months, for example. Do not slight your other studies, but make anatomy of first importance during that period. Then select some other subject, such as pattern, and concentrate on that. When you look at a picture, enjoy the color and everything else that has gone into its making, but study the pattern with particular intensity. In much the same manner, you can move on to other subjects, concentrating on one at a time.

? *Must a successful artist have talent?*

a Does a tire need air? It's all a matter of degree. The more talent, the more success. But I must admit I have seen illustrators without talent go to the top because of a fanatic desire to succeed. And on the other hand, I have seen students fail miserably who were loaded with that precious commodity.

Other factors are very important to the artist's success, or indeed anyone's success in any line of endeavor. You must have dedication, a fair amount of brains, and luck.

If an artist wishes to develop originality, I suggest that he search out some truth of nature, one that no

Perilous Sanctuary. Oil with casein underpainting.
Reprinted by special permission of *The Saturday Evening Post*.
© 1952 The Curtis Publishing Company

one has ever noticed before or—conversely—a common object and paint it in a highly personal and unaffected manner. In other words, I think you should "be yourself." If your art personality is magnetic enough, you will become famous.

? *What is the principal satisfaction you get from your pictures?*

a My only satisfaction is in the painting of them. Once they are off the easel the thrill is gone and disgust for what I have created sets in. Perhaps "disgust" is too strong—I mean dissatisfaction.

Then let us say someone likes the painting well enough to buy it. After the period of gloating over the check has passed, I begin to wonder whether he was a fool to buy it, or I was the fool to sell.

Ben Stahl

? *Do you think there is a consistent philosophy of art running through your work?*

a Only through that work where I have had the opportunity of doing it my way. A good painting is like the sun sending out tremendous vibrations of energy that warm and gratify. Verbal message, when it comes to painting, is a lot of baloney. However, in illustration it has its place.

? *Why do you paint and draw as you do?*

a Simply because I don't know of any other way. In life we are, or should be, influenced by God. In painting I was influenced by all those painters who were gods to me.

I like to paint forms in nature if they are exciting, but most of the time it is the urge to paint the things that I see with my mind's eye. I only go to nature to find out answers. It is a classroom, a place to study and to learn.

? *Do you see the end result of the painting immediately?*

a If I could visualize the end result before I painted it, I wouldn't bother to start. With me a painting just grows. Making the damn thing *grow* the right way is ninety per cent of the fun and the headache. You see, I never paint from life, or rather from an object. It influences me too much. Most of the time I paint from memory or from drawings. In illustration I don't fool around. I use, but do not trace photographs.

? *Are you deliberate about planning a picture?*

a It all depends on what it is going to be. If it is a good professional job of illustration, I'm as deliberate as you can get. But when I try to do a work of art—that's quite another story. Here I'm about as deliberate as a snowflake trying to find a place to land. Yet at the same time as positive (not deliberate) as an avalanche.

Night of Vengeance. Oil with casein underpainting.
Reprinted by special permission of *The Saturday Evening Post.*
© 1960 The Curtis Publishing Company

? *In the actual experience of making a picture, are you consciously expressing emotion or craft?*

a It's an emotional experience, but my reactions are based on years of concern with craft. Everybody is different. Van Gogh was emotional. Cézanne was intellectual, Sargent had skill. Rembrandt had all three qualities.

? *What would you advise the student painter or illustrator to look for in his own environment as subjects for pictures?*

a You can't tell an artist what to paint any more than you can tell him what to eat.

   If he can't tell a good subject from a bad one, he should give his brushes to the Salvation Army.

Generally though, anything that has felt the hand of man, things that have been lived with make the best picture. Choose an old pair of shoes rather than the new pair. Pick a landscape that contains the bones and dust of generations of Man, rather than land that has never felt the pressure of a human foot. Any place, or any thing, that is deeply impregnated with the spirit of Man makes good subject matter for painting.

Ben Stahl

? *What is the most important thing to know about making a picture?*

a Everything! But first, how to see, and even more vital, *feel.*

? *How important is drawing to the total result of a picture?*

a Drawing is everything, whether you do an abstraction or something very academic.

Just because that stick of wood has hair on the end of it instead of a piece of graphite, should not deny its basic purpose. It is an instrument with which to draw. But it scares hell out of many students when it shouldn't. Drawing is painting, painting is drawing.

Composition is all-important too. If your work is to be more than a recording of realistic action, you must learn to handle your figures as artistic material. You must compose them so that every element in the pictorial organization struggles with, or against, the basic lines of action you have set up in the figures.

? *What principal advice would you give to a young illustrator or student?*

a That's easy. Take criticism *graciously—*from *anyone.* He doesn't have to be a great artist. Digest it first. If it is bad, *then* discard it.

Just give your instructor a *tiny* bit of argument, just enough to encourage him to expand and tell you a lot more. But not too much, lest he say, "Why tell that fellow anything, he won't listen." Be vitally interested in *all* of the Arts. Read. Listen to great music. Go to the theater. *Study* all this, don't just expect to be *entertained.*

Last of all when your art instructor finishes telling you that you'll never amount to a hill of beans—lick his hand and then go out and prove that he is wrong.

21

HAROLD VON SCHMIDT

**22 famous
painters
and
illustrators
tell how
they work**

Photograph of the artist

Harold Von Schmidt has been called the greatest living painter of western scenes. Inevitably his work is compared to that of Frederic Remington, and always favorably. For nearly fifty years Harold Von Schmidt has been a prolific magazine, book and advertising artist. His paintings have received wide critical recognition. His reputation rests securely on a precise knowledge of anatomy and a gift for composition. Von Schmidt was born in Alameda, California, and orphaned at the age of five. He and his brothers were brought up by their grandfather, who filled them with stories of the Old West, scenes Von Schmidt later depicted in magazine illustrations and paintings. As a boy and young man, Von Schmidt worked as a lumberjack, mule skinner and cowhand. Thanks to an aunt who sympathized with his ambition to become an artist he was able to afford training at the California College of Arts and Crafts. Later he studied at the Grand Central Art School in New York City. His first assignment came from *Sunset* magazine. In 1920 he joined with a group of other California artists to form Advertising Illustrations, Inc. By the 1930's Von Schmidt was working for the major magazines of the day. Subsequently he worked almost exclusively for the *Saturday Evening Post*. In 1960, Von Schmidt was given the Society of Illustrators Medal and the Artists Guild Hall of Fame Award. He lives in Westport, Connecticut.

The Regional Picture

Loneliness, that's the story of my life. I think we grow when we are alone. I was once alone for thirteen days with two burros. There's a tremendous feeling of your insignificance under conditions like this. You put that into your pictures to give them significance, if you understand what I mean. These pictures are part of me even though they are commercial work.

I've drawn as long as I can remember. My grandfather was a surveyor and he used to make sketches in his notebook and he encouraged me to draw. But I will always remember the first time I got any recognition for being able to draw. My mother and father died when I was five and my brothers and I were sent to an orphanage to live. We went to the regular public school each day, where we were known as "the brats from the orphanage." One day in class I drew a horse on my slate and for some reason the teacher sent me around to all the rooms to show what I had done. At recess I wasn't one of the brats from

Girl in Cape. Oil.
Collection of Mrs. Harold von Schmidt

the orphanage any longer. I was the kid who drew
horses. This had a profound effect on me.

I want to awaken a recognition in people so they
may participate not only in seeing what I see but in
feeling it. It's amazing the letters you get. I got one
the other day about a magazine illustration I had
done. The woman who wrote the letter said, "Your
two pictures reflect perfectly the quality of the story
and made me see and feel what the words did not."
I think that's a swell thing.

? *Why do you love the West so much? Because it
represents a romantic world which no longer exists?*

a I love it for its color, great distances, its massive
shapes and its unusual beauty—and for the people,
red and white—it produced. I may go back someday.
I hope to end up squatting on my boot heels outside
an adobe.

When I was in my early teens, *Collier's* was
publishing the work of Remington each week as a
frontispiece to the magazine. These illustrations

218

meant a great deal to me. And so did Charlie Russell's work portraying the American scene, and his comments on my efforts.

But the earlier western painters did subject matter in terms of a scene, whereas I organize subject matter according to a point of view.

I've tried not to sentimentalize the Old West. Besides, there are too many people who know the West who would catch me up if I did.

Harold Von Schmidt

? *Your style is unique. Did you deliberately set out to acquire a particular way of painting?*

a Style comes not from developing a style, but by constant painting until you acquire a style. What you are will come through. Original style is essential to an illustrator for long-term success. But the ability to draw is the important thing. If you can draw well and construct a painting, you can do almost anything. As the work itself becomes your signature rather than the name you put on it, the more frequently art directors will turn to you.

The painter should take on that which interests him. If it's portraiture he should paint people. If it's landscape he should do that. Anything is paintable. It's not the subject that is important, but how you interpret it that makes it worthwhile.

Art means to me awareness. When you step out of the door in the morning and you think to yourself, "What a beautiful day!" you must remember the beauty of that first impression so you can paint it.

Seeing is the most important thing of all. Few people can really "see." They may see their hand as a hand but they don't really see it so that they can understand it. I get such pleasure out of seeing so much. The world is constantly changing and always stimulating.

I remember a man asking me on the ferry crossing San Francisco Bay, "Does an artist see differently from most people?" I asked him to look out the back of the ferry boat and then turn around and tell me what he saw and I would do the same. All he could remember was the skyline of San Francisco. I asked him if he hadn't noticed the zigzag wake of the boat, the smoke coming out of the stack, the flock of gulls overhead, the color of San Francisco, which was a sort of blue-gray, and the quality of the whole scene, a kind of wind-whipped beauty. He said, "You saw all that?" He was amazed, but an artist *has* to sharpen his eye.

219

White Bull. Oil.
Collection of Mrs. Harold von Schmidt

? *Are you excited when you begin to make a picture, or have you made so many that you approach each new one in much the same fashion?*

a I try to plan the idea behind each picture as emotionally as possible and paint it as practically as possible. I try not to waste a brush stroke. I may begin by looking through my files for research material that will help in the construction of the picture. Or I read a book about the subject. I make color notes and little sketches. And I refer to my notebooks. I have hundreds of them and they are filled with drawings. You see, these books represent a kind of artistic shorthand. When I'm riding on a horse or plane or train and I see something that interests me, I sketch it, noting the colors and the location and the perspective. Then I have something to refer to when I begin working on the details of a picture.

The painter can shoot with a shotgun, but the illustrator must use a rifle. He must be able to direct your interest to what he finds important in the story. Even if the story is a dud, you can always find something in it that interests you. You have to, because if you are not interested, how can you interest others?

**Harold
Von
Schmidt**

? *How long a workday do you usually put in?*

a At least eight hours. Very often I'll work thirty-six hours at a stretch. I get a week and a half to do a *Post* picture and that means getting the research, the models, and then doing the painting. One time I had worked for three days steadily on an advertising illustration and it had to be in New York at a certain hour. I drove in so tired I could hardly see.

I stopped for ice-cream cones to keep up my energy along the way. Finally I rubbed one in my eyes to keep awake. On the way home I pulled over to the side of the road to sleep at last, and a cop woke me up to see if anything was wrong. When he saw the chocolate circles around my eyes he thought I had been in a fight.

? *What is the most important thing a young painter should learn about making pictures?*

a He should know how to draw and something about color and organization. In commercial work skill is most important.

He should study the tone and color of the subject. Then he should doodle small sketches to find out the best way to express whatever moves him. If you tackle the big picture, first you get lost trying to hold it all together. But if you start small you familiarize yourself with it as you go along.

I think talent is a great asset but some important artists have gone a long way with intelligent hard work and great understanding of the craft of painting.

When I was starting out, I worked all day in a studio. I went to school three nights a week, taught two nights a week, and did illustrations for *Sunset* magazine over the weekend. You have to study hard if you want to do professional work. You must be able to do this kind of work with the confidence which only comes from having learned all of the elements that comprise the craft, or art, of painting.

? *How, specifically, did art school help you?*

a Well, in those days we drew from plaster casts. For example, we learned how the nose flares. We learned how the muscles come over the shoulder. We learned to mix colors. All of this is very important. I went to several schools because I thought I needed a lot of training to do what I wanted to do.

Ambush. Oil.
Reprinted by special permission of *The Saturday Evening Post.*
© 1949 The Curtis Publishing Company

? *What makes a picture come off—makes one respond to it?*

a Something painted in such a way that people understand it, appreciate it, and want to buy it. I expect to get a feeling that the man enjoyed making it. Because you can tell when he had trouble. When his subject stirs him and he has accomplished his purpose, you can tell that, too. I look for a kind of meeting of the minds. If I look at the picture and can find no way I would like to tinker with it and try to improve it after having painted for forty-seven years, that's art. It is completely realized. I always look at a painting to see how it is made.

? *Do you ever look at one of your finished paintings and have the urge to change things in it?*

a My wife hung one of my pictures in the dining room and I made her remove it. I told her that every time I looked at it I stopped eating and began to repaint the picture. Someone once said that it takes two

people to paint a picture; one to paint it and the
other to take it away from the painter.

? *What working artist would you most like to collect?*

a I wouldn't like to collect any one painter because
I would be limiting the appreciation I get from seeing
different painters solve problems in individual styles.

Harold
Von
Schmidt

? *What do you think is the cause of an antagonism to
modern art which prevails in some circles?*

a It is strange to us and we are, therefore, critical of it.
We don't always understand it. It's so easy to think
you are being fooled. Obviously the artist sees
something you don't see—yet.

? *How would you define good realistic art?*

a Good realistic art is the organization of space and the
solids within it in terms of tone and color.

? *And what is illustration?*

a An illustration is a salesman for a story.

? *And good abstract art?*

a Good abstract art has the same qualities as realistic
art because good painting is organization. Cézanne is
the father of modern art because he was the first man
consciously to change forms around to fit some
specific organization. Good abstract art must have
organization. He showed us a new way to break down
forms. Cézanne once said, "The passion that
permeates any square inch of a painting should
permeate the whole."

? *What first arouses your curiosity when you look at a
painting or an illustration?*

a I look first to see how it is made.

? *You don't have an emotional response to it?*

a That comes later. But the thing that interests me
personally is how the artist does it. I must satisfy my
curiosity on that score before I can simply enjoy
the picture.

Indians. Oil.
Reprinted by special permission of *The Saturday Evening Post.*
© 1948 The Curtis Publishing Company

? *That goes for any type of art?*

a Yes. Good abstract art must have organization too.

? *What do you think about the statement "I like it but I wouldn't want to hang it on my wall?"*

a There are a lot of girls who interest me but I wouldn't want to marry them.

? *But you allow yourself to be interested?*

a Certainly. You may not understand a painting because the artist sees something you don't yet see, but such a painting need not be suspect.

? *Should everybody try to sell what he paints?*

a Not unless he has to make a living.

? *By the word "art" do you include advertising design, furniture design, fashions, and other commercial forms?*

a A poster or a package can be art. Look at the Toulouse-Lautrec posters and the Paul Rever bowls. The artist raises these forms to the level of art.

? *Do you think it is important for America to encourage the training of young illustrators?*

a Yes I do. Ours is an industrial society dependent upon advertising. Art is a form of communication which is essential to advertising and to the health of our economy.

Harold Von Schmidt

? *If you had to choose a different kind of art training than you had in the beginning what would it be?*

a I wouldn't necessarily want a different training. But if I were starting my career today I would try to get all kinds of training. The artist must be disciplined in many techniques and know how to use all manner of media. He can then have confidence in his ability to meet any and all assignments.

? *You're a man who has ridden the range, played championship Rugby, sailed, hunted, and fished. Isn't painting rather confining work for someone with your need for physical action?*

a I've taken more of a licking from a canvas than from any of the activities you mention. Making it come out right is an emotional and physical workout. Everything requires a decision. That's the trying part. Where do you put the color? How do you use the brush stroke? I think that anyone who paints will find that through art he acquires a broader vision, greater interests, and permanent gratification. His life is richer if he paints.

? *What satisfaction do you get from your work? Is it your private fulfillment as an artist or the public response to your work?*

a I have seldom done a thing that I didn't get satisfaction from. I have been very lucky and a great many people have helped me along the way. I am happy that people like my pictures and buy them so I can do what I have spent my life doing with such enormous pleasure.

22

JON WHITCOMB

**22 famous
painters
and
illustrators
tell how
they work**

Photograph of the artist

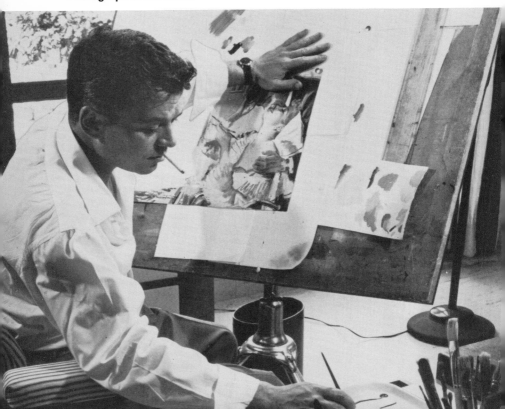

As a glamorizer of pretty girls, on stage and off, Jon Whitcomb is unequaled. His "Whitcomb girl" has become an institution in magazine and advertising illustration. Movie stars and debutantes yearn to have their portraits painted by Whitcomb. He is, in fact, as much at home in Hollywood as in his Connecticut backyard. Jon Whitcomb was born into a family of artists. His father was a drafting instructor and his mother was an art teacher before her marriage. Jon and his three sisters drew and painted as soon as they could sit up. When Jon was six, the Whitcombs left Oklahoma, where the children had been born, and moved to Wisconsin. Thanks to his informal art education at home, Jon was able to paint posters, during summer vacations from Ohio Wesleyan, to finance his education. He took his fourth college year—and his degree—from Ohio State, where he worked on campus publications. After college he got a job in a Cleveland art studio. Whitcomb understudied the older artists and eventually graduated to full rank as an illustrator. When the Cleveland studio opened a Manhattan branch, Whitcomb happily transferred to New York. Soon he was working for the major magazines—*Good Housekeeping, Collier's, McCall's, Ladies' Home Journal, Cosmopolitan, Redbook,* and *The Saturday Evening Post.* The war interrupted his career. While Whitcomb served as an officer in the Navy for three years, the field of illustration changed. He changed direction, too, when he returned to civilian life. He traveled more, going on location for pictures. He began writing books. And, he began painting more and more private portraits to satisfy the demand for his work.

Popular Illustration

I don't think talent is something you come with at birth. It is something that evolves as you live and work. About the only thing you are born with is the capacity (or lack of it) for operating. Everybody has a laziness coefficient, but successful artists have energy above and beyond what most people have or would be willing to invest in a job. The biggest successes are the ones with absolutely unquenchable energy. They have motors inside that they've never even used. I should point out though that drive is separate from your energy level. Drive comes from a deep deprivation when you were young. Most adult people who have drive have been compensating for an early lack.

The Foof. Oil over tempera.
Reprinted by special permission of the *Ladies' Home Journal.*
© 1961 The Curtis Publishing Company

You must have energy if you are going to be a hard worker. But you have to know where to apply that energy. You have to notice everything. I divide most of my friends into the noticers and the non-noticers. If you are a noticer, your antennae are up getting signals and letting you know how best to apply your energy.

? *What about style? Do you think it can be developed? Does it emerge spontaneously or is the artist's style more or less molded by the demands of the art market?*

a You don't develop a style. A style descends upon you. After thousands of attempts to do something a style evolves. It isn't something you develop. You don't have any volition in the matter. To take another example, after you play the piano for a while you develop a style that both your friends and your enemies can recognize.

If you do anything consistently you develop a kind of originality, but you aren't conscious of originality when you first start playing the piano or drawing pictures. People gradually acquire style, an individual way of working. Of course, being too original can be a disadvantage. Clients associate a certain style with you and are reluctant to let you try something else.

? *There is supposed to be a "Whitcomb type of girl."
Do you unconsciously draw the same girl over and
over even though your model may be different?*

**Jon
Whitcomb**

a Everyone has his own idea of how people look. I don't
suppose anybody sees a face the way another person
would. The pictures I do represent my personal view,
not somebody else's.

Portraits are supposed to "look within," but in my
opinion very few people have an interior significantly
different from the outside package. I have been
proved wrong, of course. Occasionally I have run
across girls who look *femme fatale,* but who were
mundane underneath. And there are also girls who are
wholesome looking but who are real rascals.

Movie stars are another matter. They know
precisely how they want to look to the public. When
I did a series on Hollywood stars for *Cosmopolitan,*
my purpose was to reinforce the image the public
already had of these stars. I was attempting to portray
their corporate movie-star images, so to speak.

? *Do you think it's true that the typical American-girl
look is going out of style and that a more
international beauty is becoming popular?*

a I think variety is high style now. Luis Estevez has
said the great beauty is a "one-woman United
Nations." I tend to agree with him.

? *How important is fashion in illustration?*

a No one seriously concerned with modern illustration
can ignore styles, whether in clothes, furniture,
architecture, landscape gardening, or picture framing.
Every year one of these gets a thorough overhaul and
illustrators have to start fresh. You have to keep up
to date if your work is to have a contemporary look.

You have to try to guess the trend that's coming up.
Since magazines work four to six months ahead of
publication anything can happen to public taste
between the time you turn in your illustration and the
magazine hits the newsstands. You try to spot future
trends by looking at what is in the popular magazines.
Of course I have my own preferences when I look at a
picture. So does everybody. I don't always like the
new trends. However, you can't do anything about
that. For example, I never liked the beehive hairdo
but it was very popular.

Love Is a Crooked Thing. Oil over tempera, gesso board.
Reprinted by special permission of the *Ladies' Home Journal.*
© 1960 The Curtis Publishing Company

I have worked out one formula which may help a
beginner forecast trends. First you must know what
the public is beginning to like. Then you analyze
what you are beginning to like. Next you decide what
you and the public both like. Imagine, finally,
what you would like even more. You may be on the
track of a trend.

? *Can you predict a coming trend in terms of a reaction
to the existing one? If, for example, hats are worn
by everybody now, won't there be a hatless period
within a year?*

a Not necessarily. You can predict this much. When hats
are being worn a lot then nobody is very interested in
hairdos, and vice versa. Public personalities influence
fashion and beauty trends. After Mrs. Kennedy
became the First Lady, her style of dressing, her way
of going without a hat, set a style trend. If you want

to know the hairdos and dress design that are going to
be popular in a few months you should be aware of
what style-setting public figures like.

? *What kind of research do you do to make sure that
the girls in your illustrations are going to look like the
popular national image six months from now?*

**Jon
Whitcomb**

a I do a lot of research so that I will come as close as
possible to projecting the right image. I'm as specific as
I can be and not just about the American look. I once
illustrated a story about a French exchange student
and I wasn't sure what she would look like. I called
the model agency and asked them if they had anybody
who looked like a French exchange student. They had
a French model who had just arrived to work for
them. She came to the studio and I sketched her and
we had a long talk about what they were wearing in
Paris that spring and how the hair styles over there
were changing.

I used to go to Paris to see the collections. This
way I was very much ahead of the fashion market in
America. I knew Jacques Fath well and Jean Desses.

? *What qualities must a good model have?*

a As far as models go, the most useful ones to use when
you are illustrating fiction are the girls who have no
private faces to get in the way of your own
interpretation. You want girls who aren't characters.
A photographer would choose a model for quite
another reason. A good photographer's model must
have a certain identity. I think it's always fun to spot
a well-known model like Suzy Parker in an ad.

? *When you are doing a portrait of a movie star you
don't want a face with no character, do you?*

a No. The hardest stars to draw are the ones with the
least character in their faces. The easy ones are girls
like Natalie Wood. She always looks like Natalie
Wood. Elizabeth Taylor is easy to draw.

? *What about Marilyn Monroe?*

a I was always so exasperated by the time she arrived for
the sitting that I wouldn't say it was easy. But she
had strong ideas about what she looked like. She knew
all she had to do was throw her head back and moisten
her lips and half close her eyes. Then she would be in

Jacqueline Kennedy. Oil. *Cosmopolitan,* April, 1961

the right pose. Some stars are like that. They know exactly how they should look. Joan Crawford is the prime example. She can tell when the light is right and when the camera angle is wrong. Marlene Dietrich is another who has this sense of herself and how she looks.

? *What if you are just drawing a pretty girl without the aura and character of a movie star? Isn't there the chance that she will be pretty but not very interesting?*

a This used to be the case before the illustrator used photography in his research. Every artist tended to do the same girl over and over. It was his dream girl. I suppose I'd do that if I were left to my own devices.

? Jon Whitcomb

? *Do certain media become popular among artists because there is a fashion-inspired trend toward using them?*

a Yes, I think one can be influenced by a trend but I don't believe you should be. I painted in oils when I was in school. But when I came to New York, everyone was working in transparent wash because that was fashionable. Later you had to do drawings in gouache or tempera.

I was rather advanced in technique when I came to New York. I was working in collage and that's very fashionable now. I had sold a magazine cover which was a pasted-up collage and that brought me to New York. I got an assignment from the B. F. Goodrich Company and they wanted me to use the same technique. And then I got an assignment from a fashion magazine where I had to draw on actual cloth. At that point I decided that drawing was more important than these special techniques. I think you should use the medium that best suits what you, personally, want to say. For example, I have begun working in oils recently because I do so many portraits. Now I do everything in oil because I enjoy the medium.

? *You say that you didn't seek an art career, that it just "happened" to you. Could you explain what you mean?*

a I suppose I didn't take art too seriously, because it was something I'd been used to. Both my parents taught art. All of us kids drew. It was just something we took for granted. I drew for my college magazine at Ohio State. Milton Caniff was there at the same time and we were reprinted a lot by *College Humor.* I majored in English and composition in college. I also wanted to be a musician and I did a number of arrangements. I still love music.

When I got out of college the first job I was offered was one painting posters, so I took it. Then I went to work in a commercial art studio.

? *In recent years you have had considerable success painting portraits. Can you tell me how much preparation goes into a portrait and how much time does it take you to make one?*

a I did an oil of a woman in California not long ago. I went to California to make color sketches of the room where the portrait was to be hung. The room was paneled in pale bleached ash and this was to be

Other People's Mail. Pastel over gouache on canvas.
Reprinted by special permission of the *Ladies' Home Journal.*
© 1960 The Curtis Publishing Company

the only painting in the room. The subject didn't
know what she wanted to wear for the picture. We
picked out three possibilities and I photographed her
in color around her house. I didn't know how much
background should be introduced. Then I came back
to Connecticut and I made some sketches. She
surprised me by picking the one I liked best, but
thought she would be least likely to choose. I could
then proceed.

I went back to California the second time and
I borrowed a photographer's studio so I could light
her really well while I took more pictures. Then
I discovered that they used only red roses in the room
where the portrait was to be hung. This meant one of
the colors in the picture had to be red.

I came back east and started the portrait. It took
me a month to paint it, but they were very well
pleased with it.

? *Do you think the artist has to sell himself even if his work is good? Does he have to tell client or art director that he is great? Is this part of success?*

Jon Whitcomb

a When you come in with a piece of work and say, "This is the greatest," it's easy for them to agree. Many people are never exposed to this idea of promoting yourself. If you don't have self-confidence, you're never going to make it. You've got to sell yourself to yourself, though, before you can sell anybody else.

I think in a great many ways the accepted social behavior for children is the antithesis of being a business success. I was brought up to be a gentleman and not brag or boast. I had to learn to fight my own shyness. I have to force myself to go in to an art director and make these reckless claims of confidence. I'm convinced, though, that you should always bring your work in person, never send it third hand. You are there on the spot to discuss any changes the client may want you to make.

? *What would you say about the opportunity to be original in advertising illustration? Some artists say it is a strait jacket.*

a From the earliest days, from the beginning of my career, I have been indoctrinated with the point of view of the client. You give the guy what he wants to buy. But for the last few years clients haven't always known what they wanted to buy. They may settle for color photography instead of illustration. But color photography has limitations. It can't transcend reality the way an artist's brush can.

This period right now offers the absolute golden era for originality. If you can come up with a new gimmick clients are waiting for it.

? *Are you satisfied with the work you are doing now? Are you consciously getting a message across to a specific audience, a message beyond the sales message in the ad?*

a Like most artists I can think of eighty million ways to do it better when I finish a picture. But you never get that chance, unless you are doing a series. All the artist can do is try to share his own vision. Apparently the reason my work has sold is that my view of the life around me has been something people have liked to look at.

Will Barnet

Arnold Blanch

Paintings and Illustrations

Austin Briggs

Stuart Davis

Adolf Dehn

Stevan Dohanos

Albert Dorne

**Paintings
and
Illustrations**

This volume
is set in Baskerville and
Univers types

The format and binding were designed by
Bradbury Thompson

The book was composed and printed by
Van Rees Book Manufacturing Company

It was bound by
Van Rees Bindery
of New York City

The text paper is
West Virginia Pulp and Paper
Pinnacle Offset, cream white

DATE DUE

AG 8- '66	JY 12 '73	
NO 9 '66	AG 20 74 m'	
NO 29 '66	6 P'	
DE 7 - '66		
MR 1 '67	MR 12 '79	
MY 21 '67	ILL	
MY 24 '67		
NO 30 '67	JUL 1 4 2005	
AP 22 '68		
NO 27 '68		
NO 27 '68		
FE 17 '69		
MY 13 '69		
OC 13 '69		
NO 20 '69		
DE 3 - '70		
MY 10 '72		
MR 7 '73		PRINTED IN U.S.A.